CHARLESTON
a Bloomsbury house & garden

CHARLESTON
a Bloomsbury house & garden

QUENTIN BELL & VIRGINIA NICHOLSON

photographs by ALEN MACWEENEY

F

FRANCES LINCOLN LIMITED
PUBLISHERS

Frances Lincoln Limited
4 Torriano Mews, Torriano Avenue, London NW5 2RZ
www.franceslincoln.com

Britsh Library Cataloguing-in-Publication data
A catalogue record for this book is available from the
British Library.

ISBN 978-0-7112-2370-7

Set in Goudy by Frances Lincoln Limited
Printed and bound in China by Kwong Fat Offset Printing Co. Ltd

5 7 9 8 6 4

Contents

Preface

by Virginia Nicholson

My father Quentin Bell was eighty-five when he started writing this book about Charleston. His memoir *Elders and Betters* had come out in 1995 and might well have been thought to constitute his last word on Bloomsbury, but Quentin could never bear to be idle, and when Frances Lincoln proposed a book about Charleston illustrated with photographs by Alen MacWeeney (who knew the house well and had photographed my family for his book *Bloomsbury Reflections*), Quentin undertook to write the accompanying text.

By the summer of 1996 he had presented a first draft. But by this time he could hardly eat and was growing increasingly feeble. In November it became necessary for him to go into hospital; when I visited him there he was worrying about the second draft and asked me to help him with the work he had taken on. During his final weeks, when he could not write, I sat by his bed at home near Firle and we talked about his memories of the house where he had spent so much of his life. I placed a tape recorder on the bedside table. The day he died he was too weak and tired to talk much to me and I realized his last book would be left incomplete. Between them, my mother and the publishers encouraged me to take on the task of finishing it.

So this book is a composite, with our respective contributions indicated by our initials. I have tried to leave intact Quentin's own writing and his own voice, transcribed from those tape recordings, and reported in quotation marks within my text. Much of the original draft needed restructuring. But it was also necessary to expand on what was in places threadbare material. My mother fortunately found a number of files with unpublished writings by Quentin including a variety of reminiscences about the house which I have been able to use. I have wrapped this original material around with my own memories and perceptions, and I have also woven in writings by a number of participants in the Charleston scene including my grandmother Vanessa Bell, my great-aunt Virginia Woolf, my aunt Angelica Garnett, and our old family friend Frances Partridge. The result may be patchwork, but I hope it is colourful.

Books about historic houses often dwell on the contents rather than the inhabitants. Because this one was written by someone who lived in the house, the associations and memories and day-to-day experience of simply living there lend an immediacy and emotion to the aesthetic experience of Charleston. In the dining room for example, there is the dumbfounded hilarity of the company presented with eleven grouse for a dinner party in 1935 when T.S. Eliot was guest of honour, contrasting with the forebodings of 1939 which overshadowed Duncan Grant's preparations to decorate the walls. In the walled garden, memories of the stricken Vanessa weeping over her dead son taint its loveliness with a terrible poignancy, but here too Quentin remembered actually crying with laughter when his mother read aloud to them from *Alice in Wonderland* one summer evening.

For me, Charleston was a holiday house. Until I was eleven our family spent part of every summer there with my grandparents and Duncan Grant, and today, no matter how often I return, the memories come flooding back – memories of adventures around the pond, of being painted by Vanessa and Duncan in the studio, of the lovely smells of new cake, books and turpentine that pervaded the house, of crocks of wet clay in the pottery, of dahlias in the garden and sweet lavender drying in spare rooms.

Above all, Charleston was a place where, for both children and adults, messy creativity was a way of life. My brother and sister and I grew up, as did Quentin and his siblings, with the conviction that Art was something everyone could do. Paint and clay, mud, glue and matches, were all endlessly available. Yet did the inhabitants of Charleston ever really grow up? There is a wonderfully uninhibited, irreverent quality to the decoration of the house which is that of a child let loose to experiment and which is extraordinarily liberating. Part of the exhilaration that people experience from looking at the brilliantly colourful

Above *Quentin in his old bedroom at Charleston in 1986*

designs that crowd the Charleston walls and furniture, comes from that sense of confidence and fearlessness. The Charleston artists did not deal with caution. What if the surfaces weren't properly prepared? What if there was rising damp? . . . Duncan and Vanessa were undaunted by such considerations. Their creative wells never showed any signs of drying up, so if the table top decorations wore out, they could always just paint some new ones on top.

I feel profoundly lucky to have been Quentin's daughter, and in working on this book I have learnt a great deal about him, about his milieu and about Charleston. If anything, I have come to admire him even more than I did during his lifetime. I feel proud to have had the opportunity to try and understand something that meant so much to him and I hope he would feel that I have justified his faith in me when he asked me to help him with his work.

Dramatis Personae

In attempting to give an account of Charleston in the twentieth century it has been necessary to mention a great many names, some of which will be well known to the reader, but some of which may not. The following brief guide attempts to characterize some of the more frequently occurring names in the text, most of them being from the circle of friends and acquaintances generally known as 'Bloomsbury'.

Before World War One 'Bloomsbury' consisted of a loose group of artists, writers and intellectuals, many of whom had first met at Cambridge University, and later gathered at the London home in Bloomsbury of Thoby Stephen, his sisters Vanessa and Virginia, and their younger brother Adrian, the four children of the eminent Victorian man of letters, **Sir Leslie Stephen** (1832-1904) and his wife **Julia Stephen** (1846-95).

Vanessa (1879-1961), the eldest of the four, a pivotal figure in Bloomsbury and at Charleston, was a painter and decorative artist; in 1907, after the death from typhoid of her brother Thoby, she married his friend **Clive Bell** (1881-1964), who became an influential art critic. They had two sons, **Julian** (1908-36) and **Quentin** (1910-96). Thereafter the marriage faltered and finally became one in name only. Vanessa had a short but liberating affair with **Roger Fry** (1866-1934), artist, critic and apostle of Cézanne and the Post-Impressionists (who remained a close friend and constant visitor to Charleston until his death). She then fell in love with the painter **Duncan Grant** (1885-1978), with whom, despite his homosexuality, she formed a partnership which lasted for the rest of their lives. Their daughter **Angelica** was born at Charleston on Christmas Day, 1918.

Vanessa's sister **Virginia** (1882-1941), now known as one of the most imaginative and creative writers of the twentieth century, married another of Thoby's Cambridge contemporaries, **Leonard Woolf** (1880-1969), who became a socialist, a literary and political journalist and a publisher, as well as the guardian of his wife's fragile health. The Woolfs had a country cottage at Rodmell, seven miles from Charleston.

When she moved there in 1916 Vanessa's household at Charleston consisted of her two young sons, Duncan Grant and his friend the novelist **David ('Bunny') Garnett** (1892-1981), both of whom as conscientious objectors refused to fight in World War One. Meanwhile, Clive Bell, also a conscientious objector, spent the war years at Garsington, the Oxfordshire home of the flamboyant patroness of the arts, **Lady Ottoline Morrell** (1873-1938). When Clive visited Charleston he was often accompanied by the elegant and sociable **Mary Hutchinson** (1889-1977) with whom he had embarked upon a long and serious affair.

Other Charleston 'regulars' from the Cambridge/Bloomsbury connection included Duncan's cousin **Lytton Strachey** (1880-1932), whose book *Eminent Victorians* made him famous overnight in 1918; **Desmond MacCarthy** (1877-1952), the literary journalist, and his family; the novelist **E.M. Forster** (1879-1970) (a closer friend of the Woolfs than the Bells); and **Maynard Keynes** (1882-1946), who was to become a celebrity as the founder of the economic theory which bears his name. After his marriage to **Lydia Lopokova** (1892-1981), a Russian ballerina of the Diaghilev company, the Keyneses took a lease on a neighbouring Sussex farm, Tilton.

Of the younger generation, **Barbara Bagenal** (1891-1984), who had been a student at the Slade Art School, was an eager, though not always welcomed, Bloomsbury acolyte. A more popular visitor was Bunny Garnett's sister-in-law, the writer and naturalist **Frances Partridge** (b.1900).

Any account of the inhabitants of Charleston would be incomplete without a mention of **Grace Higgens** née Germany (1904-83), who spent fifty years of her life devoted to Vanessa's household, the last thirty-five as resident cook and housekeeper at Charleston.

The Memoir Club *was painted by Vanessa in 1942. The club met for the first time on 4 March 1920, its members being roughly those of the original Bloomsbury group. There were no rules, and there was an understanding that members were free to say anything they pleased. By the time this group portrait was painted, three of the original members - Virginia Woolf,* Lytton Strachey and Roger Fry - *had died, so they are represented by their portraits. Seated below, left to right, are Duncan Grant, Leonard Woolf, Vanessa Bell, Clive Bell, David Garnett, Maynard Keynes, Lydia Keynes, Desmond MacCarthy, Molly MacCarthy, E.M. Forster and Quentin Bell.*

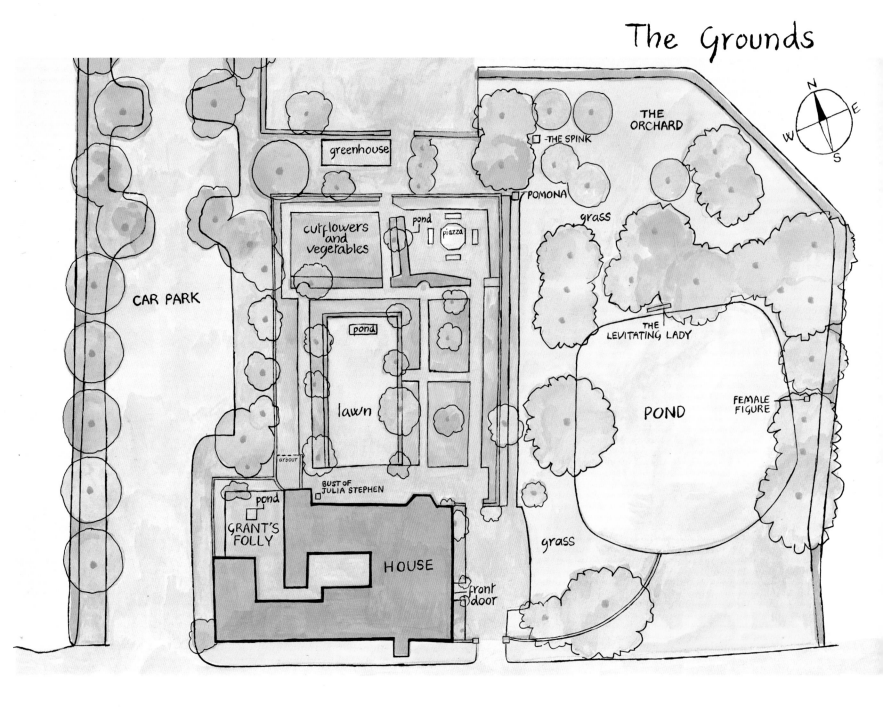

The Grounds

N
E
S
W

THE
ORCHARD

THE SPINK

POMONA

greenhouse

grass

CAR PARK

cutflowers
and
vegetables

pond

piazza

pond

THE
LEVITATING LADY

lawn

POND

FEMALE
FIGURE

arbour

BUST OF
JULIA STEPHEN

grass

pond

GRANT'S
FOLLY

HOUSE

front
door

The House

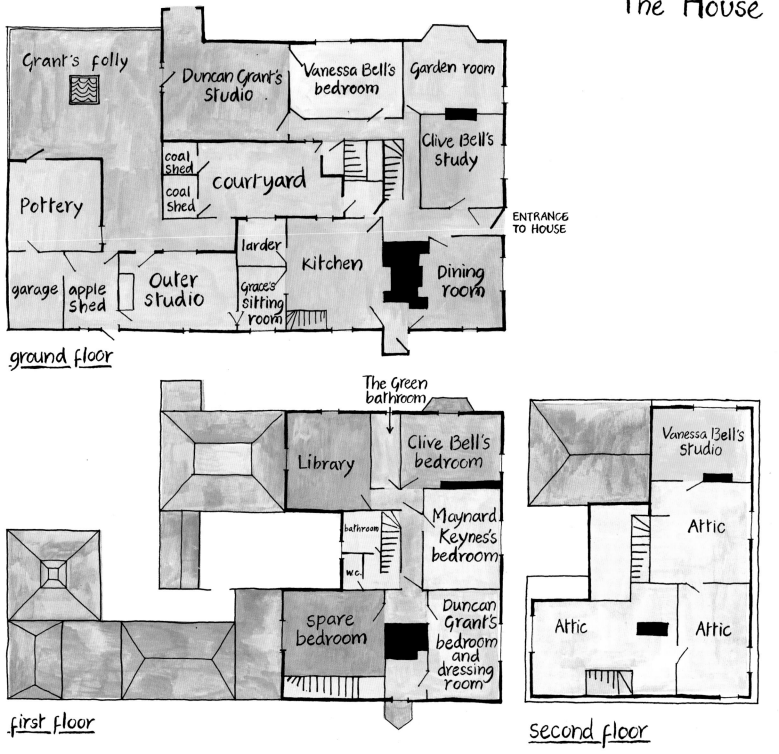

ground floor

Grant's folly

Duncan Grant's Studio

Vanessa Bell's bedroom

Garden room

Clive Bell's study

coal shed

coal shed

courtyard

Pottery

ENTRANCE TO HOUSE

garage

apple shed

Outer studio

larder

Grace's sitting room

Kitchen

Dining room

first floor

The Green bathroom

Library

Clive Bell's bedroom

bathroom

Maynard Keynes's bedroom

w.c.

spare bedroom

Duncan Grant's bedroom and dressing room

second floor

Vanessa Bell's studio

Attic

Attic

Attic

A Vanished World

by Quentin Bell

'I wish you'd leave Wissett, and take Charleston,' Virginia Woolf wrote to Vanessa Bell in May 1916. 'Leonard went over it, and says it's a most delightful house and strongly advises you to take it. It is about a mile from Firle, on that little path which leads under the downs. It has a charming garden, with a pond, and fruit trees, and vegetables, all now rather run wild, but you could make it lovely. The house is very nice, with large rooms, and one room with big windows fit for a studio. At present it is used apparently as a weekend place, by a couple who keep innumerable animals, and most of the rooms are used by animals only . . . There is a w.c. and a bathroom, but the bath only has cold water. The house wants doing up - and the wallpapers are awful. But it sounds a most attractive place - and 4 miles from us, so you wouldn't be badgered by us.'

It was Virginia who, seeking quiet, discovered the possibilities of Sussex and found refuge in Firle. There she took a very ugly house, but soon came upon Asheham, a place of great beauty a few miles to the west and in a remarkably fine situation. There, in 1912, Vanessa and most of Bloomsbury joined her. It became the summer home of the two sisters and their friends.

Then came disaster. Virginia for a time was mad, and in 1914 Europe also went mad. By 1916 Virginia was sane enough to live a quiet and normal life in Richmond and at Asheham. Europe, on the other hand, was madder than ever. In England men had to fight or to farm. This lunacy had a profound effect on Vanessa, for her lover Duncan Grant and his friend David Garnett had to choose between going to prison or working on the land. They had been cultivating raspberries at Wissett Lodge in Suffolk, but to the official mind the cultivation of raspberries was, if not positively unpatriotic, insufficiently bellicose. The soft fruits of Wissett would not save the young men from gaol. And so, when Virginia pointed out that Charleston lacked a tenant and a neighbouring farmer found that he lacked 'hands', Vanessa was interested.

One dark October afternoon in 1916 Mr Sutton's aged but capacious taxi arrived at Charleston carrying Vanessa, Julian and myself (aged nine and six), a nurse, a housemaid, a cook, Mr Grant, Mr Garnett, and Henry (who was a dog). No Mr Bell, however, for by that time Clive's marriage to Vanessa was one in name only, and he spent the war at Garsington, the home of his friend Lady Ottoline Morrell.

I think that we boys had been hoping to find something like Asheham; we did not. Asheham was a gothick building of the year 1810, standing at the head of a valley with tall trees on either side. A strange, beautiful, uncanny place, a haunted house if ever there was one. Charleston, a solid rectangular building of uncertain date, stands on a gentle eminence and looks out over the Weald. It is built in the vernacular style of the region; it is a decent and sensible place without any ghosts. To be sure there were places where, on a dark winter's night, a child taking his candle upstairs to bed might walk hurriedly past dark entries and hum a military tune, but there was nothing terrifying as Asheham could be terrifying even in broad daylight. In my youth, when questioned about the age of Charleston, we used to say that it was

'You really must come and see this place soon,' Vanessa wrote to Roger Fry in October 1916 'It's most lovely, very solid and simple, with flat walls in that lovely mixture of brick and flint that they use about here, and perfectly flat little windows in the walls and wonderful tiled roofs . . . We are just below Firle Beacon, which is the highest point on the downs near, and except towards the downs the ground slopes down from the house on all sides.'

probably eighteenth or perhaps seventeenth century. But much later on when the family had gone and the house was receiving radical treatment, a large area of the north façade had to be stripped. Under it we found a late Elizabethan half-timbered structure. Charleston is perhaps about as old as Hamlet.

Whenever Duncan and Vanessa entered a house there was a fifty-fifty chance that they would cover the walls with decorations. At Wissett Lodge they had painted a great deal and then, realizing that the householder would be distressed by what they had done, painted it out. The history of their work as mural painters is one of enthusiastic painting followed by ruthless obliteration. When in the 1950s their manner went out of fashion, the work of deletion was so thorough that today practically nothing remains save the interior of the church at nearby Upper Berwick, and Charleston itself. At Charleston the work of decoration began almost at once.

For many years almost the first thing that the visitor to Charleston would have noticed was the porch, which jutted out upon the gravel in front of the house. And perhaps the second thing would have been the Virginia creeper which grew all over

the front of the house. The creeper was removed after a long struggle in the 1930s; the porch went in 1946. Otherwise there has been no startling change. The gravel, the lawn and its bushes, the pampas grass, the façade of the house are the same. The gate into the garden is flanked by square pillars which have now been crowned with concrete urns. A great willow tree by the pond has gone, but has been replaced by a less spectacular successor. The pond itself is smaller, and the punt, the fish, the eels which in thundery weather used to bury their heads in the mud and wave their tails madly in the air - they too have gone. The orchard has acquired a population of statues but otherwise has changed very little. Beyond it lay the paddock. This for a time was grazed by a donkey, and a few years later supported an old army hut above the door of which someone had written 'Les Misérables'. This served as a studio.

The walled garden has changed almost beyond recognition. When we arrived it contained fruit trees and some potatoes and practically nothing else that I can remember apart from what had once been an earth closet. This was at its south-west corner and is now part of the studio. It was here that the artists made their first attempt to change the character of the garden. Mr - he was then I think Captain - Bagenal, who had married Barbara Hiles (one of those whom Molly MacCarthy called 'the Bloomsbury Bunnies'), accompanied by me, went into the ploughed field and collected flints. These formed the pavement in front of the earth closet. Barbara brought tesserae from London, and a mosaic was set in the pavement. Above it was a pergola. This supported a vine which had its roots in what is now 'Grant's Folly' and was then the chicken run. The chicken house abutted onto the coach house - later the garage - which faced the dairy and other farm

Left *The entrance to the house from the farm track is through a close-boarded wooden gate, painted blue-grey. In 1952 Quentin cast the urns which stand on the pillars either side of the gate.*

Right *'The pond is most beautiful, with a willow at one side and a stone or flint wall edging it all round the garden part, and a little lawn sloping down to it, with formal bushes on it' (Vanessa to Roger Fry, 16 October 1916).*

Vanessa with her three children, Quentin, Angelica and Julian in 1920, in the walled garden beside a plaster cast bust, which is no longer there.

buildings. Walking down the road and past the wash house (later my studio), one passed the kitchen window and the kitchen porch and returned to the garden gate. In the wash house, which contained a great fireplace and several coppers, was the pump which drew water from the same source as the pond - but not in that first winter. Then everything was frozen solid and we had to cross the fields with buckets to the one spring that still flowed.

On the steep and flinty gradients of the downs where horses could not plough, there were still oxen in those days. In Lewes, a

child could buy a pound of black gunpowder, for there still were farmers who used the old muzzle-loaders. And there were some who dared not shoot a hare for fear that it might be a witch (I fancy that there still are).

The old coach road to Alfriston had become a green lane but was still used by the grocer's horse-drawn van from Firle. The new main road bent and twisted like a hooked eel; there were no buses on it and very few private cars. When the Charlestonians visited Asheham they walked or bicycled. Visitors from London took the taxi from Lewes or Berwick, or walked from the station sending their luggage by 'Happy Jack's' milk float. But this could lead to delays, for if he saw a policeman, Jack flung down his reins and made for the downs where he might stay for days. He, like the Charlestonians, disliked the idea of military service.

In the house, there was of course no telephone, no radio, no central heating. Sometimes a child might bathe in a tin hip-bath set before the dining room fire. There were paraffin lamps, one of which set fire to the beam in the dining room ceiling - you may still see where it hung - but one went to bed by candlelight.

But although Charleston was in many ways behind the times, we children believed ourselves to be very well informed. We were interested in politics and in the progress of the war. I can date that bath in front of the dining room fire from the fact that Vanessa and my nurse were discussing the news of a second revolution in Russia. And then our governess had a relative who knew someone who was on some general's staff (I seem to remember that a lot of people had relatives in this position). But even this informant, who for a long time assured us that victory was inevitable, seemed insignificant when compared to Maynard Keynes. Maynard came from the very hub of government. He talked to Lloyd George as you or I might talk to Happy Jack. And Maynard was even more optimistic than the person on someone's general staff. And he was even more interesting about the peace than about the war.

Peace, when it came, was disappointing. It brought a Christmas present in the form of a sister, Angelica, the child of Vanessa and Duncan, but it failed to bring plenty. We children had expected iced cakes, chocolates, hot baths. The soldiers would come marching home in scarlet uniforms and splendid busbies. And in fact we did have a tiny glimpse of the *dolce vita* in London, whither we were sent to enjoy a feast of culture offered by Diaghilev, and one of more substantial delights provided by Buszard's tea-shop. Perhaps we abused that opportunity, for we were sent back to Sussex under the care of a nurse who, after one night at Charleston, repacked her bags and fled. There was no coal, little wood, no butter, no meat, and no hope in the house. Upstairs Vanessa and the new baby were both very ill. The peace celebrations at Firle were damp and dismal.

As soon as it was possible, Vanessa and her three children moved back to London. Charleston now became our summer home. In the years that followed Maynard, Duncan and my father were with us and became regular summer residents. That at least was the intention, but our landlord Mr Stacey (who was himself a tenant of Lord Gage, on whose estate Charleston stood) had other ideas. In the summer of 1924 Vanessa, accompanied by me, visited my brother Julian who was now at school in Reading. She told us that it seemed we should have to find another country home; she was looking for a house somewhere in East Anglia. I think it was then that we realized how much we had come to love Charleston.

How she worked it I do not know, but somehow Vanessa managed not only to remain there, but also to negotiate a much longer lease. It was then that Maynard named her 'Ludendorff Bell'. This arrangement, which was to endure for the next half century, had a profound effect upon the structure of the house. At different times during the ensuing years the larder became Vanessa's bedroom, the larder itself being accommodated next to the kitchen. Adjoining the kitchen, a new room for the use of those who worked in the kitchen was made, connecting it with the wash house. More dramatic was the construction in 1925 of a large studio which incorporated the mosaic-paved pergola (i.e. the old earth closet). Beyond this the chicken run became 'Grant's Folly'.

What I think of as the golden age of Charleston lasted for about twelve years, from 1925 to 1937. Perhaps a list of the guests who came there may give an idea of the company we kept. Apart from the obvious people - the Woolfs from Asheham and later from

Duncan felt a natural affection for small children and animals; the cousins here are Judith (the daughter of Adrian and Karin Stephen) and Angelica.

Rodmell, the Keyneses from Tilton over the way, and Roger Fry who planned the new studio and designed the walled garden - there were Lytton Strachey, Desmond and Molly MacCarthy, Raymond Mortimer, G.E. Moore, Frances Marshall (later Partridge), William Plomer, T.S. Eliot, Janie Bussy, André Dunoyer de Segonzac, Jean Renoir and Charles Mauron. The list could be extended. Later Julian brought F.L. Lucas, Anthony Blunt, Harry Lintott, Eddie Playfair, John Lehmann and a great many other Cambridge friends.

Vanessa's photograph albums express her love for friends and family. The 1920s, when she took these pictures, were the 'golden age' of Charleston, before the convulsions of the 1930s brought unrest and, later, tragedy. **Above** *from left to right: Frances Marshall (about whom Angelica composed the lines: 'Then there's Miss Marshall, to whom we are partial'); Quentin; Julian; Duncan; Clive; Beatrice Mayor (an old friend and playwright). In front are Roger Fry and Raymond Mortimer.* **Opposite top left** *In the early 1920s, when this picture was taken, cars were rare events at Charleston. David ('Bunny') Garnett is the driver of this glorious vehicle.* **Opposite top right** *Clive; his mistress Mary Hutchinson; Duncan and E.M. Forster. When he visited Charleston in the 1920s, Quentin took Forster to be the plumber come to mend the boiler.* **Opposite bottom left** *Clive and Lytton Strachey in the walled garden.* **Opposite bottom right** *Top row: Auberon Duckworth (Vanessa's nephew); Duncan; Julian; Leonard Woolf; bottom row: Virginia Woolf; Lady Margaret Duckworth (the wife of Sir George Duckworth, Vanessa's elder half-brother); Clive; Vanessa.*

On a fine day one would discover Clive with a few friends comfortably seated on the gravel in front of the house, enjoying the sunshine, *The Times*, their conversation and sometimes even the books that they were supposed to be reviewing for the *New Statesman*. But a certain number were tempted to the studio either to paint or to be painted. I have lively memories of Desmond MacCarthy enthroned as a model. We had the double pleasure of taking his portrait and of listening to his immensely attractive voice as he read Henry James aloud. That memory at least is communicable, but how can one reproduce the conversation of that vanished age? It was free but never naughty or bawdy. I only once saw Vanessa shocked, and that was when a guest declared that Titian could not draw.

That happy time ended in 1937 when my brother was killed in the Spanish Civil War. During the months which followed, Charleston seemed the saddest place in the world. By the time Vanessa was sufficiently recovered to lead a normal life, it was

Above *Vanessa, Duncan and the co-author Virginia aged about five. I was not much older than this when my grandmother died, but Vanessa's relationship with her grandchildren was a charming and imaginative one, not easily forgotten.*

Opposite *The north front of the house, seen from the far corner of the walled garden. The upper window was added in 1939 to light Vanessa's studio.*

clear that another war had become inevitable. Clive and the artists decided to make Charleston their full-time home for the duration of the conflict. Clive brought his books and furniture from London. A new bathroom was made and served, not from the spring, but from a reservoir; mains water was followed by electricity. The vestiges of the old hen house in Grant's Folly became a pottery. The house thus acquired its present shape and the last major work in the garden was completed.

As a wartime refuge Charleston had much to recommend it. With a farm next door, a garden full of produce and a countryside rich in game, we did not starve. If some bombs and infernal machines intended for London fell upon us, we could hardly grumble. Our real peril arose from the possibility that a German army might cross the Channel. That would have been the end of us, for we lay upon their proposed line of advance, and although Private Bell armed with a shotgun and Private Grant who had a rifle of so old a vintage that it would take no known form of ammunition were a source of entertainment, they would not easily repel the German army.

But a disaster of this kind became less and less probable, and victory eventually arrived. Charleston itself was hardly affected by the war. Rather, it spread its influence when Berwick Church was decorated in the 1940s. This was the last joint commission that the artists would receive. In the late 1930s Vanessa, and even more Duncan, had gained a considerable reputation. But the time of their prosperity was short. During and after the war newer and younger painters attracted attention, and in the post-war period they were almost totally eclipsed. Unable to sell pictures they had painted, the Charlestonians sold some of those they had bought. As each one left the house it was commemorated with a copy. Thus when the big Vlaminck went from the drawing room, Vanessa made a copy which she signed with a 'V'. But when Duncan's supposed J.F. Millet was identified as a genuine Poussin, no copy was made.

Under the circumstances, Vanessa might be excused for being depressed, but despite the death of her sister Virginia in 1941, she faced the post-war years with considerable equanimity. Angelica, who had married David Garnett, produced a bevy of girls who were able to enjoy the pleasures of Charleston, which for children are considerable. This great source of comfort was increased by the advent of three more grandchildren. This brought the further pleasure of getting them, for the modest fee of sixpence, to sit for the painters.

Vanessa died in 1961 and for a time Duncan and Clive lived very amicably at Charleston, but in 1964 Clive also died. This left Duncan alone there, with Grace Higgens, who had worked for us from 1923, to look after him. The attempt by Grace and her husband, who had done wonders against increasingly impossible odds, to look after a house which by now was largely uninhabited and very damp, was in the end defeated. And finally Duncan himself had to move to the house of a friend, where he

Right *The front hall contains a typically disparate range of furniture; an Italian mirror and Italian painted chairs, flanking a nineteenth-century Chinese lacquered table; on this is seated the Chinese God of Earth. The Chinese objects were mostly introduced to the house by Julian Bell, who spent two years in China in the 1930s. The handbell was used to summon people to meals.*

Opposite *The hall and passages were undecorated by the artists, in contrast to the surprisingly rich colour of the principal rooms. Here the view into Clive's study reveals the window embrasure decorated by Vanessa around 1916. During the restoration of the house, the conservators were faced with immense problems in trying to preserve such spontaneous and fragile designs as these.*

died in 1978. For a short time Angelica lived at Charleston and made heroic efforts to deal with a situation which had, in fact, become impossible.

If Duncan had not lived so long I very much doubt whether Charleston would have been preserved for posterity. By the 1950s Duncan's art was considered out of date; but the cyclical movement which seems to govern the taste of an age meant that by the 1980s he was venerated. Charleston too, which had been the absurdly over-decorated toy of those preposterous Bloomsburys, had become part of the cultural history of our century.

This evolution of taste was made much more powerful by the intervention of Miss Deborah Gage (a relative of Lord Gage), who organized, inspired, and animated the body which became the Charleston Trust. This aimed to ensure the repair and restoration of the house, raising the funds, instructing and supervising the work of an army of builders and specialist craftsmen. Miss Gage, a delightful and energetic young woman, inspired everyone to achieve wonders. In addition it was she who, in the words of

Canning, called in the New World to restore the balance of the Old.

At last the work was done - the house repaired by very careful hands, the garden blooming and considerably better tended than it had been for the last seventy years or so. We opened our doors to the public and waited for a visitor. We had been told that a few people, perhaps as many as half a dozen a week, might come to Charleston. It seemed a reasonable estimate. Then we discovered our error. The public came 'not single . . . but in battalions'. Our devoted band of guides was almost rushed off its feet, and when a special day was appointed for the great, the good, and the erudite, they too seemed almost too numerous. Our carpets wore out, and when we provided a gallery for exhibitions and a shop and a video machine, they served only to increase numbers.

Charleston, which began as the refuge of a small band of highly unpopular refugees and developed as a centre for the small society of Bloomsbury, has become a popular institution, a kind of time capsule in which the public can examine a world which has vanished.

Clive Bell's Study

QB This, surely, is the proper place at which to begin, not because it is central in the house, although it is that, but because we are concerned here with architectural cosmetics. The face of Charleston is to be painted and it was here, in what is now the study, that the mistress of the house first took a brush and, with a few sure-handed strokes across the window embrasure, brought Charleston into the Post-Impressionist world.

I think we may safely assume that until this first assertion of a new age upon its walls, the house had hitherto known no more unconventional wall decorations than, perhaps, a bold spread of new ivy leaves papered across an upstairs room. Who can say? But from this time and for a very long period afterwards Charleston was to undergo drastic changes, and when Virginia Woolf made an occasional visit she nearly always found a joyous chaos with pots of paint on the floor.

There was no thought then of it being Clive's room, and it may have been years before he even saw the interior of what was to be his study. It was the family living room.

Charleston being a horribly cold house, especially during our first winter there in 1916-17, Roger Fry designed a big rectangular fireplace intended to throw more heat into the room. It was constructed with iron braces and firebricks by Bunny; the design was echoed in the garden room and still is. The fire in this room became a sort of kiln when we children played there. We had found a nice vein of blue clay near the pond and this could be modelled into bricks, pillars and domes and buried in the fire. Here it would either explode or emerge hardened and changed to a lovely salmon pink. With these it was possible to build houses, streets, temples, palaces and, of course, fortifications. The floor of the room would be transformed into a theatre of war.

We gathered around the fireplace for tea every evening and were joined by Duncan and by Bunny Garnett at the end of their day on Mr Hecks's farm. Tea was taken with a confection called marrow jam, the vegetable marrow being made more palatable - that at least was the intention - by being flavoured with ginger. I never conquered the dislike of vegetable marrows and of ginger which I then acquired. I remember also from that time the division of butter. It provided a fairly small ration which had to be supplemented by margarine. Such were the delights of home life during World War One.

By Christmas 1918 I remember that this room was occupied by us boys and by Mrs Brereton our governess as a schoolroom. It was here that my brother, looking through the window from without, once saw her kissing her lover. That Christmas Mrs Brereton must have taken a short holiday. On Christmas Eve the doctor who had come to supervise the birth of our sister arrived. We boys were left unattended and invented a game in which we pretended that the room was Rome and that we were the Gallic invaders. We sacked Rome and in the process fatally damaged

Roger Fry's ingenious hearth design now contains a primitive electric fire. The armchairs either side of the fireplace are, on the left, an antique French chair upholstered in a fabric entitled 'West Wind', designed by Duncan, while the one on the right is covered in 'Abstract', designed by Vanessa. Both fabrics were printed in 1931, but these are Laura Ashley reproductions. The bookcases mainly contain Clive's collection of art books. Above the one on the left hangs Duncan's 1959 painting of Charleston's farm buildings. Clive (aged twenty-seven) surveys the room from above the right-hand bookcase in a pencil portrait by Henry Lamb of 1908. The central canvas is Still Life with a Bookcase, *painted by Duncan in 1919.*

Left *Vanessa decorated the fire surround with bold circle motifs in 1925-26. Under Duncan's supervision, Nerissa Garnett, Angelica's daughter, distempered the walls green in 1971. What Quentin described as 'a figure of great antiquity and some charm', a plaster cast whose origins are unknown, stands on the mantelshelf.*

Right *Vanessa's decorations on the window embrasure were done in 1916-17, at a time when this was a family living room. The low table in the window was made by J. J. Kallenborn, a cabinet maker frequently employed by the Omega workshops. The potter Phyllis Keyes provided a number of the house's ceramic objects which were decorated by the Charleston artists, including these tiles set into the table top, decorated by Duncan in the 1920s or 1930s.*

the lower part of the door. As a result the door is now decorated by Duncan with panels of two very different dates. The following day we were banished to Asheham to stay with Aunt Virginia.

Staying with our aunt was a wholly undeserved treat for us and no doubt something of a relief for the inhabitants of Charleston. For them it was a wretched time. The baby began to pine away and the doctor inspired no confidence, Vanessa was ill, and Mrs Brereton and the cook lived in a state of undeclared war. The hardships and privations of the war seemed to be intensified by the peace and, as soon as possible, Vanessa moved herself and her family to London. Charleston then became a summer residence.

When we did return for the holidays the grown-ups thought it better to move into the drawing room proper, which in the summer months gave ready access to the walled garden after dinner.

Occasionally after the war Desmond MacCarthy borrowed this room as a study, that is to say that he was in the room, with materials appropriate for the production of literature: paper, ink and anything else that the muse might require; also on one occasion that I remember well, he had a handbell. This he needed because his health was bad, he was getting very old and might need help. I was in the room above and therefore when I heard the bell, I was downstairs at once.

'My dear boy,' he said, 'I need some fire water.' I brought him some whisky and he gave himself a generous amount; in front of him was a pen and a ream of virgin paper. He had all the impedimenta with which to write but, as so frequently happened, he found the business of writing impossible. What he did now have was an audience, and that was all that was needed. He could not write, although no doubt there was an editor to whom he had promised an article, but he could talk and talk. Even then, when he was old and unwell, his talk was magical.

Clive's study did not finally become Clive's study until, in 1939, he moved all his books and much furniture from London.

VN After breakfast Clive would generally retreat here to read *The Times* and to write; he was an excellent correspondent and some of his best writing is probably in his private letters to Mary Hutchinson, Raymond Mortimer and Frances Partridge. He seems not to have much enjoyed the process of writing, being a

Above and opposite *The two panels of the door to the study were decorated by Duncan at different dates, the lower panel having been smashed by Julian and Quentin when they used the room as a schoolroom. The upper panel dates from around 1917 and incorporates motifs from the house at that time. Duncan painted the acrobat below in 1958. To the right of the door stands a large Provençal cherry-wood cupboard, c. 1780; on it stands a weathered plaster cast of a Classical head, recovered from the garden wall. Many of the poetry books on the shelves to the left of the door belonged to Julian Bell and were brought back from Cambridge by him.*

perfectionist who in a curious way wanted to write without having to bother about writing; it did not come naturally to him. He sat down, calmly, with plenty of pens and inks arranged in an orderly fashion on the nineteenth-century Dutch-style marquetry table which had been a present to him and Vanessa on their marriage in 1907. When his implements were assembled he would set to work. His handwriting was as clear as typing, with each letter separate, and when he had written a first draft in black or blue he would then carefully correct it in red ink.

Clive greatly admired Horace Walpole and strove to imitate Walpole's 'set phrase', his technique of the 'art of observation'. He was always looking for the perfect quotation. Such literary mannerisms presented a negative example to his younger son, who set out deliberately to reject them in his own writing.

Henry Lamb's portrait of Clive which hangs above the bookcase to the right of the fireplace shows him as kindly and urbane. To his young sons Clive was a benign, though rather absent father, but he had a good relationship with his boys. When Quentin was a young man he yearned to be more like him, for his easy worldliness and success with women represented everything that Quentin felt he himself could never achieve. But after the advent of Hitler, Clive and his sons never again saw the world from the same viewpoint. Clive's fear of war led him to try and find arguments in favour of Fascism. 'It was a kind of moral blindness . . .' which after the war drew him into a position of strongly reactionary politics. He became intolerant and quarrelsome; 'he couldn't bear me to be a socialist'.

But overall, though I suspect he felt no great filial love towards his father, Quentin was charitable towards Clive's weaknesses, and remembered him as a kind and placatory parent: 'Once as a child I saw Clive really angry, as one seldom did. I had stolen his red ink and used it for I know not what naughty purpose. I was appalled by what I had done, so much so that I walked to Firle (not a very long walk) and purchased a fresh bottle of red ink in the village shop. Clive's anger had long subsided by the time I came back with my bottle of red ink, and we were friends again as we almost always were. I hope I was equally forgiving when my own children misbehaved.'

Above *Angelica, Clive and Quentin standing on the gravel terrace outside Clive's study in 1922.*

Right *The nineteenth-century Italian gilt mirror in the hall reflects a view of Clive's study through the open door. On the mantelshelf, behind the plaster figure, a black-and-white photograph is the only reminder at Charleston of Duncan's Poussin landscape, which he bought in Paris for £40. (Clive told people, 'We think it is by one of the many artists called Millet.') Its true worth was not recognized until Anthony Blunt identified it in 1964. He bought the picture from Duncan, who was perennially hard-up, though years later, rather to Duncan's chagrin, sold it on to the National Gallery of Montreal for a much larger sum.*

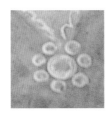

The Dining Room

QB It was in the dining room, seated at a square table which is now in the kitchen, that my formal education began with lessons from Vanessa. I knew how to read before coming to Charleston but I learnt or, to put it more exactly, I was taught to calculate at Charleston. It is extraordinary what parents will do when they become pedagogues. Leslie and Julia Stephen made the most dreadful hash of their attempts to teach Vanessa and Virginia, and now Vanessa, the kindest of parents, reduced me to tearful despair with the multiplication table. Do other children feel pleasure, grief and fear when faced with the multiplication table? Do they feel an intense hatred for the number seven, and a certain quiet affection for numbers ten and five? I learnt to dread arithmetic in this room, while feeling perfectly happy with very elementary attempts to learn a few words of French. All my schoolroom emotions, it must be added, were heightened by the presence of an intelligent and sometimes aggressive older brother.

I do not think that Vanessa persisted in her attempt to teach us for very long, when, in 1917, our nurse and nursemaid departed. They were replaced by Miss Eva Edwards, a trilingual governess and a young woman who, so I later discovered, was more interested in the sentimental possibilities of Mr Keynes and the other gentlemen, than in her little charges, who, it must be said, did once attempt to throw her into a ditch.

Miss Edwards was replaced by Mrs Brereton. I got on well with her, but Julian did not. Mrs Brereton had I know not what family links with the church and was a staunch Christian. Julian, who was conscious of the family links with our agnostic forebears, took the opportunity to revive old disagreements about the historical character of the book of Genesis, and for a time the arguments and perplexities of the nineteenth century raged between him and Mrs Brereton to the sound of distant gunfire from across the Channel. This could be heard quite distinctly in March 1918; the German offensive on the Western Front was so deafening that it made the windows facing the garden in this room rattle in their frames. I remember them rattling again in the summer of 1940, but I do not remember them doing this at any other time.

At a time in the mid-twenties when Roger Fry was planning the new studio, the Victorian iron firegrate and its surrounds in the dining room were removed and the room greatly enlarged by the revelation of a large open hearth in which there is room for two seats. The fire itself was lit within a round opening under a brick chimney-breast, which had a small gothic niche set into it. Roger had come to convalesce at Charleston after a bad attack of influenza. He sat after lunch on one side of the fire, Vanessa on the other, looked at the gothic arch and told Vanessa that it was very ugly. Then he asked Vanessa for a cold chisel and a hammer. It was hard work for an invalid but, with a little help from her, he changed the shape of the niche. It looks very well.

The round table came to Charleston in 1934. Vanessa's first decorations on it wore out and her new ones are now wearing in

The red lacquer and cane chairs are from the Omega Workshops and were designed by Roger Fry in 1913. Quentin made the ceramic lampshade which hangs over the centre of the table when he took up pottery in the late 1930s; the small holes pierced in it throw patterns of light on the ceiling. Flowers, c. 1911, by Roderic O'Conor, is visible between the windows. O'Conor had been a friend of Clive's in his bachelor days in Paris. The dining room is hung with curtains made from floral chintz. Vanessa used this fabric, often in contrasting strips, to sew curtains for several of the rooms in the house.

Left *In 1918, when* Interior *was painted by Duncan, the dining room served other functions besides eating; it was also a living room and schoolroom, hardly recognizable from its appearance today. Here Vanessa, on the left, has set up her easel, while Bunny Garnett, on the right, is writing. It could almost be the scene described by Virginia Woolf in her diary in March 1919 when she visited Charleston and found it in a state of chaos: 'One has the feeling of living on the brink of a move. In one of the little islands of comparative order Duncan set up his canvas, and Bunny wrote a novel in a set of copy books . . .' The table is now in the kitchen, and the old fireplace has yet to be improved by Roger Fry.*

Right *When the alcove was opened up in 1925 it provided enough space for the two Provençal armchairs either side of the chimney breast. In the niches are two English nineteenth-century flower vases, and a Staffordshire figure stands in the central niche which Roger Fry constructed. On the mantelshelf is an array of plates collected by the painters on their travels in Europe.*

their turn, particularly at the end - if a round table can be said to have an end - where she habitually sat to serve the food.

The stencilled wallpaper was Duncan's idea although I performed much of the mechanical side of the business. I think that it had a sedative effect which at that time was very helpful to both of us. His plans for redecoration coincided with the politicians' preparations for war in 1939. As instructions were issued to the population to carry gasmasks, so Duncan began to make ready his large stencils and bowls of paint, and as the situation in Europe grew worse and worse, the extremely hand-made stencils extended across the black walls.

VN As in many rooms at Charleston, the decoration was carried out rapidly and without due preparation. As the house was leased, permanency was not the most important consideration. The work was carried out with reckless spontaneity on top of many existing layers of paper, and this in due course made restoration extremely difficult. Duncan and Vanessa both made their own stencils out of paper, using a sponge to apply the paint. They used colours which in those days were cheap and easily obtainable; unfortunately they were also unstable. They were based on white chalk, which gave them body. To this was added powdered pigment, with rabbit-skin size as a binding agent, though not an

efficient one as it did not entirely 'fix' the colours. As the colour dried the white chalk reasserted itself, giving a 'bloom' which is reminiscent of fresco paintings.

It was at about this time that the telephone first made its appearance in the Charleston dining room, 'after years of waiting'. There had always been arguments about whether it would be a blessing or a curse. Quentin was for progress; Clive and Duncan were against it for fear of social complications, but when it eventually arrived it proved its use immediately. About a week after it was installed, the stove in the hall overheated and the timbers in the wall against which it stood began to smoulder, and then blaze. The house might well have burnt to the ground had the inhabitants not been able to call the fire brigade. Quentin, I am sorry to say, gloated on his victory over the Luddites in an ironic verse worthy of McGonagall:

'Fast as light the call for help is gone,
It shows the value of the telephone.'

Gradually, the dining room emerged as a habitable and civilized room for family meals. Breakfast was an informal affair since people came down when they pleased. Virginia Woolf would often probe her friends and relations about even this most trivial aspect of their daily lives and would interrogate them about their breakfast as a way of satisfying her intense curiosity about people; her *cri de coeur,* 'What did you have for breakfast?' developed into a family joke. Duncan's preference was for porridge, which he ate in the Scottish manner, dipping spoonfuls into a separate bowl of milk and sprinkling it with salt. Anyone who wanted eggs or bacon had to go into the kitchen and fetch them from where they were being kept warm on the Aga. Clive, who was meticulous about his toilette, was usually the last down. After breakfast everyone would wait anxiously for the postman who also brought the newspaper. Then people dispersed: Clive would seize *The Times* and carry it off to his own room, the painters would depart to their studios and the writers to their desks.

From the early days, Vanessa liked to maintain an atmosphere of formality at mealtimes - as far as was possible with two small boys shouting at each other ('our manners were pretty ill . . .'). A small lobby behind a curtain (the fabric designed by Duncan) led through to the kitchen. The servants emerged from here bearing the food. Lunch was a hot meal on Sundays - Southdown mutton perhaps. A joint would be sent out from Marsh the butcher's in Lewes every week, and it would reappear cold on Monday and as shepherd's pie on Tuesday. For many years the family ate off the set of plates and dishes designed by Duncan for Clarice Cliff, of which a few remain on the side table. After Quentin became a potter, he provided the family with much of their crockery - the soup bowls which he made are on the same table. They drank water or beer at lunch and there would be coffee afterwards.

They were not so Bohemian in their manners as is often supposed; if there were guests, which there frequently were, the household tended to change for dinner. Beforehand, everyone would gather in the drawing room, now called the garden room, for a drink. When the handbell in the hall was rung everyone would stroll through to the dining room. Vanessa sat at the southern side of the table, where she served; Clive sat opposite. Duncan would sit with his back to the fire and the conversation would continue.

It was conversation of a kind which often fell into a pattern. According to Quentin, Clive was often the initiator. He loved to make provocative assertions, to which Duncan would rise saying, 'But you don't really mean that, Clive,' then Julian or Quentin, less naïve, would retort, 'Yes, but he does.' And so it would proceed.

Opposite above *Grey and yellow patterns on a black ground were stencilled by Duncan and Quentin onto the wallpaper in 1939. Later it had to be reproduced in places where it had decayed irreparably, this section being part of the facsimile.*

Opposite below *The first set of Vanessa's decorations on the dining room table became worn through use and she painted the top with a new design in the early 1950s.*

Right *This is one of the few original examples of fabric designed by Duncan to survive at Charleston. Entitled 'Clouds', it was, like many of Duncan and Vanessa's textile designs, printed by Allan Walton Ltd. This curtain hangs across the doorway which leads into the lobby next to the kitchen.*

Left above *These plates and dishes were in regular use at meals; they were designed by Duncan Grant in 1934 for Clarice Cliff, a ceramicist better known for her geometric Art Deco designs than for these loose, curvaceous patterns. The tea caddy is a Phyllis Keyes cast, decorated by Angelica in the 1930s.*

Left below *Quentin learnt to throw pots at the Foley works in Staffordshire in the mid-1930s, the director of Foley, T.A. Fennemore, being a friend of Duncan and Vanessa's. Quentin provided much of the family's crockery thereafter and these soup bowls were made by him in about 1938.*

Right *Above the small Venetian side-table hangs* By the Fire, *painted by Duncan in 1916 when the painters were living at Wissett Lodge, Suffolk. To the right of it is* Hotel Garden in Florence, 1909, *by Vanessa, one of her earliest extant paintings. The portrait is of Saxon Sydney-Turner, an enigmatic figure much respected by loyal Bloomsbury friends for his intellectual brilliance, but it is hard to fathom his contribution to that circle, as he is reputed to have remained mostly silent. After gaining a double first in Classics at Cambridge, he entered the Treasury where he remained in obscurity. He was musically the most gifted of the group, and this portrait of him at the piano was painted by Vanessa in 1908.*

Sometimes the discussion would continue into the coffee and brandy stage, by which time the party would have returned to the drawing room where, long before the matter was resolved, Vanessa would fall asleep in an armchair over her knitting. She loved to celebrate guests with the best hospitality she could afford. Two of them, Lytton Strachey and Saxon Sydney-Turner, both appear in portraits which hang in this room.

Most years Quentin's birthday took place at Charleston. It was in the middle of the summer holidays, on 19 August, and being a week after the opening of the grouse-shooting season was usually celebrated with grouse and audit ale, specially brewed for Cambridge colleges. His fifteenth birthday party in 1925 was memorable for the collapse of one of the guests:

QB Maynard Keynes, who sometimes provided fireworks to be let off after my birthday dinner, was present, as was Lydia (they were newly married). Leonard and Virginia Woolf were there, and so were Duncan, Vanessa, Julian and Clive. Although the room could be illuminated by lamps I think that we had candles that evening. A good deal of Trinity audit had been consumed and the party had just about reached that stage at which Maynard would oblige with a song of the 'Vive la Compagnie' description, when Virginia intervened. She was on form and brilliantly amusing. There was laughter and applause and then, suddenly, she seemed to be changing her mind, rising, making as if to move from her place. The two people who knew her best, Vanessa and Leonard, were up on their feet, racing for the door and arriving just in time to catch her as she collapsed. She was green as a duck's egg. It was the beginning of six months' ill-health brought on by overwork and a plethora of social engagements, and the clamour and merriment of that birthday party proved more than her constitution could bear.

But the night of the Great Covey was perhaps our finest hour. T.S. Eliot was a frequent visitor at Monks House (the home of Leonard and Virginia at Rodmell) but it was not until September 1935 that he visited Charleston. Vanessa had last seen him at a dinner party at Roger Fry's house when they returned home together and their conversation proved so absorbing that Eliot left the manuscript of poems he was carrying behind on the tram,

never to be seen again. So his visit to Sussex seemed a momentous occasion, an occasion for ordering grouse. Lottie, our tempestuous but enthusiastic cook at the time, could cook anything so long as it was a luxury, and grouse suited her fine. Vanessa therefore went to Lewes to order the birds, but before she left she asked for Clive's advice and was told by him that a bird between two was a fair allowance. Unfortunately, this estimate was somehow confused and Vanessa ordered one bird for each person. There were eleven of us in all, so Grace brought in eleven birds resting on various dishes and platters. There was a good deal of astonishment and some laughter when this covey made its appearance; our guest of honour the poet was delighted.

I who had never met him before, felt that I might take liberties. I took them: 'Who were Mrs Porter and her daughter?' 'Who was Sweeney?' - all the questions that Eliot enthusiasts ask themselves. Eliot was happy to explain that these were Aryan campfire myths collected by earnest seekers after truth on the Great Barrier Reef of Australia. He went on to describe a disastrous tea party, his guests being the Herbert Reads who had been surprised, but not amused, to discover small india-rubber fish in their tea, this being Eliot's device for enlivening a tea party.

He had much else to tell. He was funny, charming yet still somehow impressive. It was a wonderful evening.

Above left The Dining Room Window, Charleston, c. 1940 by
Vanessa, shows Duncan and Angelica with their coffee after lunch.

Above *On the far wall is a strongly Post-Impressionist portrait of
Duncan's cousin, the biographer and essayist Lytton Strachey, painted in
1913 at Asheham, the house a few miles from Charleston which was
rented by the Woolfs and the Bells before World War One. Lytton was a
frequent guest both there and at Charleston. The wallpaper behind this*

*painting is part of the original, restored and re-hung. Below the portrait is
an eighteenth-century English piano inherited by Duncan from his father.
The ceramics in the dining room are typical of the miscellany at Charleston
and include pots made by Quentin and Staffordshire ornaments. The
English glass cabinet in the corner of the room is uncharacteristic of most of
the furniture of Charleston; it represents a relic from Vanessa's childhood
at the Stephen family home in London, 22 Hyde Park Gate, and contains
decanters and brandy glasses from that period.*

The Kitchen

VN The kitchen is one of the few rooms at Charleston which has never changed its function, although it was very different when the family arrived in wartime. There was a cold water tap but during the first terribly cold winter of 1916-17 it froze. Quentin remembered how they used to go over towards nearby Peaklets Cottage where there was a spring which never froze, returning with jugs and cans of water. There was of course no electricity; provisions were stored in the larder which was reached down a long passageway and up a step round a corner. That state of affairs continued until 1939 when the larder was transformed into what is now Vanessa's bedroom. Then a small but somewhat more practical larder was created next door to the kitchen itself. Food was cooked on a big kitchen range stoked by coal and meals made their appearance in a rather ramshackle way. Later, the range was replaced by an Aga stove.

Although Vanessa was capable of cooking, and sometimes did so, she always employed a cook, in order to have the freedom to paint and to spend time with her children and friends. After breakfast she would go into the kitchen to order the meals, then she would go off to her studio at the top of the house and leave the cook to get on with it.

Groceries were delivered from Flint's the grocer who had a shop in Firle; their smart little horse-drawn van made its way along the old coach road under the downs and brought supplies. They had hens at Charleston so it was easy to get eggs, and the farm also had a dairy. All the vegetables grew in the garden, Bunny Garnett kept bees for their honey, and sometimes people went foraging. Blackberries grew abundantly close to the house, and over towards Asheham, on top of the downs, the children used to go and pick the wild raspberries that had self-seeded there.

Inevitably the need for Vanessa to employ domestic servants, so she could work and survive the rigours of bringing up her family, led to the complications which so often arise between maid and mistress. Domestic crises loomed large in their lives as Vanessa's correspondence often reflects: '[Jenny] left the larder in such a state that I had to spend all yesterday morning cleaning it out . . . How I hate these domesticities. I can't conceive what the female mind is made of' (Vanessa to Duncan Grant, 29 July 1919).

'I won't write any more about servants. I'm feeling as if I'd rather do all myself than have these to-dos. Their conversation is more exhausting than that of all the intellectuals in London' (Vanessa to Virginia Woolf, 3 July 1918).

However, while Vanessa clearly suffered from the vagaries of her domestic arrangements, her children were frequently entertained by the eccentric behaviour of the Charleston staff:

QB My first memories are of the Zany, a nice, quick girl, but aptly named. Vanessa was giving Julian and me a French lesson in the dining room when the Zany came in quietly saying: 'Please mum the cock's laid an egg.' There was a pause for silence and reflection, then she left. She was unreliable but in no way unpleasant, and fortunately not unreliable when she came into the drawing room saying, 'Please mum the house is on fire.' It was. Everyone liked the Zany but in the end she had to go.

Although the family never ate here, the kitchen is now a cheerful and convivial room which is often used for entertaining. A large oil-fired Aga stove keeps the kitchen permanently warm, summer and winter. It replaces a pre-war solid fuel stove. The blue-and-white willow pattern serving dishes on the mantelshelf are a relic of Number 22 Hyde Park Gate, the London home in which Vanessa, her sister Virginia and their brothers grew up.

An assortment of cups made by Quentin hang on hooks beside the pink door which leads to a boxed-in staircase. This rises two floors to the attic where the servants slept. It was known as 'High Holborn', a whimsical reference to the London thoroughfare running to the south of Bloomsbury. The ceramic and bead lampshade was made around the time of the restoration of Charleston by Victoria Walton, a friend and pottery assistant of Quentin's, in imitation of the house style.

She was followed by Mrs Pitcher, the cook, and her husband. Their reign was during the rather longer epoch of our governess Mrs Brereton. It is, I believe, traditional for the governess to hate the cook. The tradition was observed on both sides and the Pitchers withdrew. At what stage Trissie made her contribution I am not sure, but Trissie was socially ambitious and when she gained the affections of a young farmer in Firle, she let it be understood that she was the lady companion of her friend Mrs Bell and in no sense anyone's servant. This complicated life rather. However, Trissie married her farmer and left.

She was succeeded by someone far worse called, I think, Emily. Emily came from the slums of Glasgow and had an illegitimate baby who crawled all over the kitchen floor and who was far from clean. Emily also had a temper. When crossed she would pack some bricks in a pillowcase, and use it as a weapon to defy all comers. Even we boys found Emily a bit too much. One day she was accused of theft and Vanessa insisted on visiting her room where she found an enormous quantity of sugar (this was on the ration), and that was the end of Emily.

Then came Mary. My main memories of her are in London; she was very likeable, full of laughter and for us boys a treat. She joined us in mischief, sending hoax letters to all the inhabitants of Gordon Square telling them of a meeting at number 46, Maynard's home, to form a new tennis club. Dozens of frustrated people turned up. But Mary's hoaxes were the outward manifestation of something altogether more hysterical. The poor girl was deranged and her delusions began seriously to disrupt the household. Eventually she was led away to a lunatic asylum.

Sanity finally prevailed when Grace Germany, as she then was, joined us in London when I was about twelve. She became almost at once part of a strange triumvirate consisting of herself, Lydia Lopokova and me. The three of us would meet in the kitchen of 50 Gordon Square and Lydia, who had led an odd romantic life in Europe and the Americas, would tell us about droshkies, moujiks, boyars, the Nevski Prospekt, Holy Russia and the ballet. She would give us tickets for performances and at weekends would take me with Maynard in a hired Daimler to the Tower, Westminster Abbey and Richmond, and show us the world. Between

Grace Higgens was first employed by Vanessa in 1920, when she was sixteen. She worked for the family for over fifty years during which time she married a Sussex man, Walter Higgens, and brought up their son John at Charleston. Vanessa painted this picture of her in 1943; it now hangs in an upstairs corridor. The war-time kitchen at Charleston in which Grace stands making pastry appears amply provided with vegetables grown in the garden. The dishes on the mantelshelf still stand there today; the large refrigerator which can be seen in the background was at that time a recent, modern acquisition provided by Clive, who enjoyed such extravagances as ice in his gin. Since those early days little else has changed in the kitchen. Onions hang from hooks on the ceiling, also garlic, not a common ingredient in traditional English cookery, but Grace had picked up French habits when she went with the family to Cassis. Vanessa ordered some French dishes, such as omelettes or crème caramel, but most of the meals that Grace cooked were traditionally English. There was nearly always soup, and often plain roasts, or game for special occasions.

Above *Both the tiles behind the Aga commemorating Grace Higgens and the splashback behind the Belfast sink were late additions to the house, made by Quentin during its restoration.*

Opposite *Vanessa decorated the kitchen cupboard with flowers and fruit in the 1950s. The paintings were done on canvas to fit the door panels.*

them they spoilt me terribly and made me unfit for the world of public school that awaited me.

Did we spoil Grace too? Not exactly, but she was oddly treated. There was a time when Grace was living with us in Cassis in the south of France and was talking freely, in who knows what lingua franca, to her friend Elise Anghilante who came daily from the town. 'Northern and Southern Beauty', Clive called them. Grace's charms had to be defended with a shopping bag used as a club against the advances of the Rumanian artist Grigorescu. There was also a formal *demande en mariage* by a worthy Cassisean who, in the proper French manner, addressed himself to Vanessa as the near equivalent of a parent. But Grace resisted all attempts to make her a citizen of the third republic. She returned to England, and eventually to marriage with a Sussex man, Walter Higgens. This established her at Charleston, where she remained until she retired.

VN After World War Two Grace ruled supreme at Charleston. Under her, the household remained orderly. Furniture was dusted, floors swept, washing done and meals served at regular intervals. Vanessa brightened up the kitchen cupboard with paintings of flowers and fruit and Quentin's pottery hung from the cuphooks. Then the kitchen became a most welcoming place to spend time. The postman, who ended his round at Charleston, certainly found it so, and would convey local gossip to Grace while seated on a chair by the door with a cup of tea. Grace's battle-scarred tom cat Sam was often curled up by the Aga and an amiable mongrel called Blotto lived in a barrel behind the kitchen porch. Grace liked to bake and Vanessa's grandchildren were allowed to help her and scrape out the bowl afterwards. Sometimes at the end of the day Vanessa would emerge from her studio to cook scones in the kitchen, which she found relaxing after hard work. The small room adjoining the kitchen which had once led into the antiquated wash house was converted into a sitting room for the Higgenses where, at some point in the fifties, they installed a primeval television. Grace retired at last in 1970, and Quentin made a plaque which testifies to her devotion. It reads: 'Grace Higgens, née Germany 1904-1983 worked here for fifty years & more. She was a good friend to all Charlestonians.'

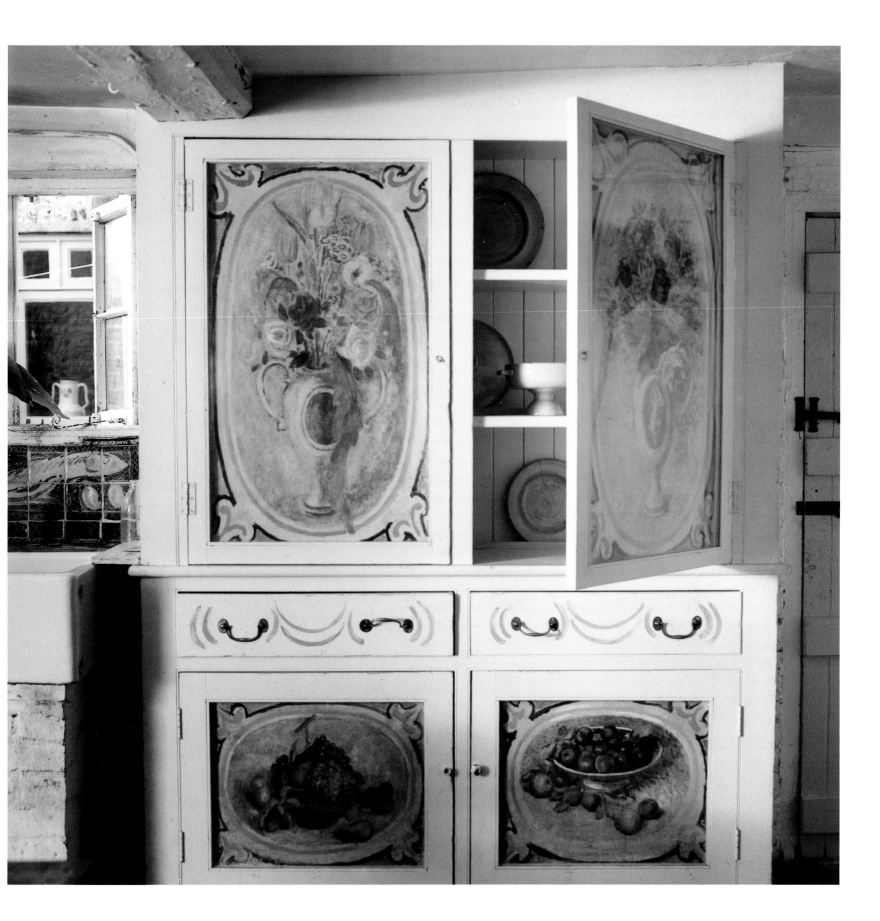

The Garden Room

QB In the very early days this charming room was not much used. Life centred on what is now called Clive's study and on the dining room, at least that was where we worked and played as children, while the garden room was used for storage. Bunny Garnett's beekeeping impedimenta was kept here, for all his life he was an enthusiastic beekeeper. The floor was strewn with the husks of the sunflower seeds which he ate, having acquired this habit during the time he spent in Russia with his mother Constance Garnett, the translator of Tolstoy. He had not acquired the habit of sweeping them up. Yet clearly the room was used, since Roger Fry found it necessary to replicate the cunning heat-projecting fireplace design of Clive's study here, while Duncan painted angels on a box to contain logs as early as 1917. And it was in that year or the beginning of 1918 that Lytton Strachey read *Eminent Victorians*, or a part of that work, to the Charlestonians. Duncan, it is said, disgraced himself by falling asleep, wearied more, I suspect, by his agricultural labours than by Lytton's reading. I also remember a later performance by Lytton in that room, when he read aloud from his play *Iphigeneia in Aulis*, not I think one of his best efforts.

One dark afternoon, in the days before electricity came to Charleston, I came into the drawing room holding in my hand an Aladdin lamp which I left on the mantelpiece next to the mirror. The heat cracked it clean across. The painted figures either side now support a floral design by Duncan which effectively replaces the original oval mirror.

Eventually the garden room was adopted as a drawing room by the adults. Its great charm was that in fine summer weather one could saunter out into the garden and have a quiet smoke or perhaps a quiet chat with the scent of flowers all around. Vanessa and Duncan both tended to fall asleep there, and if, as often happened to Clive and myself, one had some letter or other work to finish, one went upstairs to one's bedroom. If on the other hand one came down again, it was often to find that the sleepers had thwarted one by waking up and starting an intense conversation. It could be most provoking.

When Charleston finally acquired a wireless it found a home in this room. It was here in 1939 that I listened to Mr Neville Chamberlain complaining that he had really been treated very badly by Herr Hitler who had been so unkind and unreasonable. With us were Duncan's mother and his aunt Daisy. Duncan's mother was a proper *memsahib* and although she and Duncan's aunt had fled from Twickenham where they were convinced the German bombardment would be severe, she felt that her sister was letting the side down by shedding tears. 'If you're going to cry like that then go upstairs,' she commanded, and Aunt Daisy took refuge in a pocket handkerchief. It seemed to me that the poor

The figures painted by Duncan in about 1928 above the fireplace once supported a mirror, cracked accidentally by Quentin. Today they flank a basket of flowers. Below, on the mantelshelf, a charming eighteenth-century French ceramic lion smiles rather than roars. Roger Fry's home-made fireplace still survives, the mirror-image of his other construction in Clive's study; before it is the fish rug, designed by Duncan in the 1920s. The log box was decorated by Duncan at a time when he was still in thrall to the Ballets Russes. Two of the angels are dancers, the other two are musicians. The fireplace is a piece of confusing trompe l'oeil: one might be persuaded that it was of some inferior material painted to imitate stone, but beneath the grey speckles it is in fact plain marble. Little fireside tables with lamps make comfortable resting places for a book or a cup of coffee.

woman shouldn't be blamed for greeting the beginning of hostilities with tears.

In the early twenties Julian used to bring his friends from Cambridge to stay at Charleston during the summer months. Then we would all invade the garden room which had been, when we were children, the preserve of our elders and betters. It was characteristic of Julian that he and I and his Cambridge friend Eddie Playfair once spent a whole night in this room discussing the meaning of 'Good' - a discussion which I believe ended in some kind of decisive statement. The conclusion was reached at six o'clock in the morning. What it may have been I cannot say, for by six o'clock I was asleep.

VN Julian brought his girlfriends to stay at Charleston too. He had his first serious love affair at Cambridge with a young woman called Helen Soutar. She was, Quentin said, 'a very plain girl' who rather hoped to marry Julian, and who he, being promiscuous but always sincere in his promiscuity, felt morally obliged to marry. 'It would have been a disastrous thing to do.' His taste in women was erratic and was forever landing him in trouble, culminating in a reckless affair which he carried on with the wife of the Dean of Wuhan University during his time in China in 1936. Julian's love of women was equalled by his love of politics:

QB On those occasions when I went with him to Cambridge I discovered that we were regarded as eccentrics in this regard. 'The Bell brothers are members of the Labour party, they are decidedly odd!' Such was the common opinion of our Cambridge friends. And yet there came a time, just when it was I am not sure, when the attitude of young Cambridge to Julian somewhat

Left Julian Bell and Roger Fry Playing Chess by Vanessa, c. 1931, was painted from studies made in the garden room. Roger Fry befriended Vanessa's children from their earliest years, at the time when he was in love with their mother. 'To know Roger in person was a treat,' Quentin has written. 'He was patient, concerned and warm with his wonderfully deep, trembly voice . . . and he was the best of teachers for one longed to be taught by him.'

Right In the evenings Vanessa often fell asleep over her knitting by the fire. The book is Volume 1 of the works of J.M. Synge, inscribed 'D. Grant from C. B. 1913'; the cover is decorated with a collage by Duncan. The lamp is one of a pair either side of the fireplace, made from Spanish bottles.

changed. Now he was no longer condemned for taking an interest in politics, but for not being a member of the Communist party. As a distant observer I was not well informed, but it seemed that suddenly the university had turned to Moscow for its doctrines and we with our rustic socialism were more helplessly out of touch with contemporary opinion than ever.

Nor was it only contemporary opinion which found our views hard to understand. Many years later, that amiable eccentric, Tom Driberg, wrote to me apropos of I forget what historical enquiry - and asked whether it would be incorrect to describe Julian as a typical Communist intellectual. It was after all a very natural assumption. He had been a close friend of Anthony Blunt at Cambridge. And yet, in all our disputes, he attacked while I defended Communism, not that I myself was ever a Communist,

but I did deplore the enthusiasm and violence with which Julian turned against those who might have been our friends.

I hope that readers may forgive this digression into the world of politics. No account of life at Charleston in the third decade of our century can honestly omit the period of political agony which afflicted us. Had my brother Julian lived, his passions and his violent anti-Communism might, I feel, have led him into a career as a politician. Instead, he was killed driving an ambulance in the Spanish Civil War in 1937, and the garden room is always associated in my mind with the tragedy of that time.

VN 'I shall be cheerful, but I shall never be happy again,' Vanessa wrote to Vita Sackville-West at that sombre period after Julian's death. But why she chose that time to tell Angelica that Duncan, not Clive, was her real father, is hard to fathom.

Above *The French windows open directly onto the garden. Quentin recalled the pleasure of strolling into the moonlit garden on a summer night: 'Cheroots were lit and there was Haydn or Mozart on the old clockwork portable. One went out through the windows, and to Mozart was added the delicious scent of tobacco plants . . . we who had ventured out spoke in hushed voices as though in deference to the night. Eventually guests would begin to feel cold and we would return to the drawing room with its warm, shabby, comfortable armchairs, a tot of brandy and conversation.'*

Right *Above the sofa hangs Vanessa's copy of* Poissy-le-Pont *by Maurice Vlaminck, 1909. The original painting was exhibited at the first Post-Impressionist Exhibition organized by Roger Fry in 1910. Clive and Vanessa bought it from the Parisian dealer Kahnweiler in 1914. It was later sold, but Vanessa copied it first, signing it 'V'. Vanessa designed the paisley pattern which was stencilled onto the walls by her and Duncan in the 1940s. The white flowers were added freehand. The original was damaged by damp, and some of the present wallpaper is a facsimile.*

It was in the drawing room that summer, however, that she did so. Angelica has written, 'It was a fact which I had obscurely known for a long while.'

In the late thirties the household at Charleston was rocked by these convulsions and others in the world outside. Soon after the outbreak of World War Two Virginia Woolf drowned herself. But though the golden age of Charleston seemed to have gone for ever Vanessa continued to paint. With the help of Duncan, whose companionship had now become indispensable to her, Vanessa gradually recovered her equilibrium and even a measure of serenity. The quiet grey and white stencilled paisley wallpaper of this room was designed by her at the end of the war. The self-portrait which now hangs to the left of the fireplace is of a beautiful but grieving old woman, whose sad presence seems to impress itself upon the room.

Left above *The Dutch folding card table bears a cast of a 1908 portrait bust by Pierre-Auguste Renoir of his son Claude ('Coco') aged seven, which is flanked by a pair of French nineteenth-century vases. The mirror is eighteenth-century French. In the foreground is a characteristic squat lamp stand decorated by Duncan in the 1920s. It is one of a pair, of which the other is in his bedroom.*

Left *Vanessa designed the cushion cover in 1925; Duncan's mother Ethel Grant embroidered it in cross-stitch. Behind the chair is a screen painted by Duncan in about 1934. Its design of white flowers may have suggested the motif which was later painted on the wallpapers. It came to Charleston from Duncan's studio at 8 Fitzroy Street, London, which had previously belonged to Whistler and Sickert.*

Right *Though their pattern changes, the curtains and pelmet's restful colours harmonize with those of the wallpaper. Duncan designed the curtain fabric in 1931 for Allan Walton Ltd; this is the original material. The curtains were shown at the Alex Reid & Lefevre Gallery, London, in 1932-33 in an exhibition of interiors, to which Duncan and Vanessa contributed the 'Ideal Music Room'. An easy chair in front of the window contains a cushion designed by Vanessa and worked by Ethel Grant. To the left of the chair is a small table with tiles made by Quentin in the 1950s.*

Vanessa Bell's Bedroom

QB Vanessa's bedroom has remained unaltered since she died here. But before her occupation, that is to say before the remodelling of the house and the building of the studio, it served a very different purpose. It was then the larder and was in constant communication with the kitchen. At that time the window was small and protected by iron bars and the furnishing consisted of a slate shelf which occupied the outer wall. At some early stage in our occupation, someone - probably Maynard - had the extravagant idea of buying a barrel of oysters. The oysters covered the entire slate shelf in the larder and although a great many went to the dining room a great many remained on the shelf, until eaten by Julian and myself. After a time even our appetites could not keep pace with the mortality rate among the oysters, many of which had to be thrown into the pond. I remember the incident with gratitude because oysters, when not too desperately expensive, have been my favourite luxury ever since.

VN In 1939 the larder was converted into Vanessa's bedroom. The tiny barred window was replaced with a French window opening onto the garden, and a door was made communicating with the studio. A bath and wash basin were installed and a screen was

The Heal's bed is covered with an embroidered bedspread bought in Broussa, Turkey, when Vanessa travelled there in 1911 with Clive, Roger Fry and Harry Norton. The tall cupboard was decorated by Vanessa in 1917; it originally contained a foldaway bed. Vanessa's three children are the subjects of the portraits, left to right: Julian Bell Writing, *by Duncan, 1928;* Quentin Bell, *by Duncan, c. 1919;* Angelica Bell as Ellen Terry, *pastel by Duncan, 1935. This last is inscribed 'To V. B. from D. G. 1935' and shows Angelica aged seventeen dressed for her role in Virginia Woolf's play,* Freshwater.

placed to separate them from the rest of the room. The cupboard, which was decorated by Vanessa when she first came to Charleston, and the bed were moved downstairs from her previous bedroom, now the library. When she came to inhabit the room, Vanessa's passion for her family was reflected in her choice of paintings for the walls.

QB That Vanessa should be remembered as the devoted mother surrounded by her children is no doubt proper. But Vanessa herself would have been a far less interesting character if she had always been proper. There was a famous supper party in 1918, at which Diaghilev and Picasso were present, when Clive, who could be a dreadful tease, tormented Vanessa mercilessly. She tried to silence him, to persuade him to stop, all in vain. It so happened that while he was teasing her, she was serving jam tarts to the company. She took a tart, as a player might take a cricket ball and threw it with all the force that she could command so that it burst - as Maynard Keynes put it - like a shell, upon her husband's solar plexus.

The point of my story is that in taking the initiative and resorting to rather unconventional methods, Vanessa was acting in character. I do not mean that her life was marked by continual resorts to direct action, but merely that she was always ready to assert herself. In truth I do not suppose that she ever threw a tartlet at her father, Sir Leslie Stephen, although I imagine that she would have liked to have done so. Sir Leslie must have infuriated Vanessa with his constant complaints (after his wife's death) that she would ruin them all with her prodigality in running the household. She is more likely to have answered his accusations with a composed silence than with a shrewdly aimed tartlet, and I dare say that was almost equally provoking.

Left *'I am sitting at my open bedroom window . . . it opens down to the ground and I look out on to the lawn which has been extended up to the terrace - Quentin's idea for making our garden a second Versailles. The monthly roses are in bloom. It's a hot summer evening . . . the pinks are making the whole place smell . . .'* (Vanessa to Janie Bussy, 6 June 1940). *The curtain fabric was designed by Vanessa for the Omega Workshops in 1913; this is a reproduction of the original design, carried out by Laura Ashley in 1986.*

Right Interior with Housemaid *by Vanessa, 1939. This was painted soon after Vanessa moved in to her new bedroom; the figure holding the broom is Grace. Vanessa was a prolific letter-writer and her Provençal desk is cluttered with writing materials.*

Above *Vanessa outside the garden room in 1925.*

Opposite *Vanessa's desk is a nineteenth-century French fall-front secretaire. Quentin modelled the rather unconvincing terracotta likeness of his sister Angelica which stands on top. Vanessa designed the cover of her writing case; it was worked by Ethel Grant, who also embroidered the spectacle case above it on the desk. Vanessa's elder son Julian is the subject of the two studies by Vanessa made in 1908 when he was only a few months old. Although the frame containing Julia Margaret Cameron's photograph of Vanessa's mother Julia Stephen never actually stood here, it seems an appropriate place for her among the closest members of Vanessa's family. The chair is one of a set of six Venetian chairs owned by Clive.*

Vanessa was sixteen when she lost her mother, the parent whom, she had confided to Virginia at a very early date in their childhood, she loved best. Her photograph by Julia Margaret Cameron stands today on the desk in this room. Vanessa knew early on that she wanted to be a painter, an objective which her mother's family would have understood, while Virginia wanted to follow her father's profession and become a writer. Sir Leslie, much to his credit, wanted to help both his daughters achieve their ambitions. He opened his library to Virginia while he allowed Vanessa to prepare for and eventually enter the Academy Schools, where she was taught by Sargent. Just how remote Vanessa's ambitions were from anything contemplated by this man of letters may be judged by the fact that when Vanessa returned from her art school with an *écorché* (anatomical figure), her father was astonished. He had never seen such a thing in his life.

Thus the two sisters were trained in two very different disciplines and, although united by an affection which was very strong, they were divided by their very different perception of the arts. Virginia would refer to Vanessa's 'strange silent fish world' and although Vanessa found Virginia's description of the Stephen family at St Ives in *To the Lighthouse* almost unbearably moving she could also, as Virginia herself despairingly recorded, ridicule her taste in green paint.

It must be said that the bath in Vanessa's bedroom is not exempt from green paint, and nor is Charleston in general, but it was part of Vanessa's character, like her husband's, that she enjoyed teasing and had a strong sense of the absurd. The sadness of her old age often obscures the memory of more cheerful days. Nothing is more difficult than to revive the merriment of the distant past, and yet I am the only person alive who can remember the time when Vanessa was young and beautiful, the time when it was natural to think of her as someone who was always laughing.

One of my funniest memories is of Vanessa as an instructress. Julian and I were sitting with Vanessa on a garden bench and she was telling us how babies were born; I must have been four or five. The babies were inside her, she said. Julian, as usual the one with the adventurous mind, thought this out for a moment. 'In that case you must have a considerable stock of babies ready to be

Above *Lurking in the shadowy corner beside Vanessa's bedroom door, this self-portrait of Duncan was painted around 1910, when he was about twenty-five.*

Opposite *The room is divided by this striking Omega Workshops screen, painted by Duncan in 1913. It was on exhibition at the opening display of the Omega Workshops in July of that year.*

produced on occasion . . . Do you mean to say', he asked, 'that there are hundreds and hundreds of babies inside you?' I remember one of those great explosions of laughter to which I think I was prone, an explosion which set off the other two. Whether Vanessa managed to bring back the discussion to a more serious plane I cannot remember, all that remains is that impression of wild comedy which I experienced again when Vanessa read us *Alice in Wonderland* for the first time. Our odd family life was indeed one in which laughter was the predominant theme, the leitmotif. We laughed at and with Vanessa, she laughed at and with us, we all laughed at Duncan.

VN And yet Virginia Woolf once described her sister as 'terrifically monolithic and imperious - a terrifying woman in her way . . .' (*Diary*, 8 April 1935). She surely recognized something that Quentin was also well aware of, that her sister possessed a dictatorial streak. Quentin recalled, 'Vanessa was the firm pillar of our existence. She was sensible, practical, imperturbable, at times filled with a gentle gaiety, always morally and physically beautiful. She didn't talk much but she controlled everything.'

Perhaps this combination of hilarity with discipline was what made Charleston such a creative and congenial place to be. At the centre of everything was Vanessa, a woman who had, as Quentin put it, 'stared catastrophe in the face and smiled at it', reckless yet resilient, her love for Duncan surviving everything that fate could throw in her path.

Duncan's self-portrait, moody but handsome, hangs by the door. Though Duncan often strayed, being, as Quentin put it, 'rather a cold-hearted bugger', Vanessa made a milieu for him at Charleston which was so utterly irresistible that he always returned. 'For all his defects as a lover, Duncan was in her view a genius; to work with him was an honour, to be criticized by him a delight, his qualities as an artist outweighed all other gifts and graces. For the best part of half a century she managed matters so that this impossible love affair was made possible. And she had a wonderful gift,' Quentin recalled, 'like Madame de Sévigné, of turning her rivals into her friends.' Vanessa died in this room in 1961. After her death it was Duncan who wept over his own heartlessness: 'I could have been kinder to her,' he said.

Left *The bath was installed in the corner of Vanessa's bedroom in 1939; its panel decoration was carried out by Duncan in 1945; the 'Fountain' behind the taps was added after Vanessa died, in 1968. The hanging cupboard was decorated by Angelica in the late 1930s. Her daughter Nerissa, Vanessa and Duncan's granddaughter, sat (rather glumly) for her portrait by Duncan in 1965. The chair she is sitting in is on the other side of the room, under the 'Ellen Terry' portrait.*

Opposite *The naked light bulb and washbasin are unusually utilitarian in appearance, particularly in contrast to the mirror, whose wool-work frame is decorated with half cross-stitch; Duncan designed it in about 1940 and his aunt Violet McNeil carried it out. The simple marble-topped washstand is an early piece by Vanessa, from around 1917. Over the bath is a painting by Duncan of 1931, Spanish Dancer. There is no known sitter for this figure; however, the motif was a favourite, and turns up in various drawings and designs.*

The Studios

VN   Until 1925 Vanessa and Duncan had painted in the house or in an old army hut in the garden known as 'Les Misérables'. It was wretched indeed, and when Vanessa negotiated a long lease on Charleston, she and Duncan were finally free to construct a proper studio which would suit all their requirements, with room for a sitter or model. Roger Fry, as usual the *éminence grise* behind improvements at Charleston, described the undertaking in a letter to his friend Helen Anrep:

'Here we sit and shiver except when Vanessa and I are forced to go out into the backyard and try to measure the area of her projected studio with a broken tape measure, which is all that the place affords. However bit by bit we are conceiving a grand scheme and I've at last finished the plans, elevations and details. It's really the humblest architectural effort you can imagine, for the great object is to have as much room and spend as little money as possible. That of course appeals to my avaricious nature, which is almost as much gratified by saving other people's money as my own. Anyway it's great fun trying to make use of all the queer shapes of wall that these sheds and outhouses provide and drawing them together into a single building . . .' (Roger Fry to Helen Anrep, 18 April 1925).

A firm of builders from Uckfield built it onto the house where the chicken run had once been. Vanessa wrote to Roger in September of that year:

'I have been working quite hard in the studio, which has completely changed one's life here. It is a perfect place to work in, as besides having a very good and even light it is curiously quiet and removed from all the noises of house and garden . . . The stove has come and yesterday we lit it for the first time. It smoked rather but I think it will be all right. Altogether we are quite installed now and one feels for the first time here more or less independent of weather' (Vanessa to Roger Fry, 11 September 1925).

The studio that Roger Fry designed was a large rectangular chamber, the walls of which were painted with dark colours. These were chosen not for themselves, but to serve as a background for pictures. The soft tones of grey, green and dark pink were ideal for enhancing the brightness of Duncan and Vanessa's work, where a more conventionally white-painted room would have deadened their impact.

When the house was being restored it was discovered that the studio walls had, in fact, been painted only after the pictures and the large mirror had been hung. Clearly Duncan and Vanessa had never considered doing anything so time-consuming as taking them down and hanging them up again, and when they were finally removed areas of bare plaster were exposed.

The north wall is pierced high up by a long window which admits a north light. Below it hangs a series of pastels by Duncan's friend Simon Bussy. That side of the room, with its long table, was always the most businesslike area, a place for palettes, brushes and other studio impedimenta.

In later years, the studio doubled as Duncan's sitting room, being one of the warmest rooms in the house, for the Pither stove was far more efficient than the radiators which were installed in 1939; here his visitors always found something new and exciting to look at, the colours and shapes of its numerous exotic objects and images forming a remarkable harmony. The armchair beside the fire is protected from draughts by the screen placed behind it, which was decorated by Duncan in the 1930s. The armchair has a bedspread flung over it, and the cushion cover is made up - probably by Vanessa - from a French provincial cotton printed square.

Left *The large mirror reflects Duncan's Male Nude, c. 1934. The pine cupboard was decorated by Richard Shone in about 1968. On it stands a smaller cupboard, whose open doors reveal the figures of Adam and Eve painted by Duncan in 1913. The plaster cast of a head on top of the cupboard was rescued from the garden wall. In the foreground is a gramophone decorated by Vanessa in 1932. The decorative drug jar is probably southern Italian.*

Above *Duncan's tubes of paint, pastels, brushes, bottles of turpentine and linseed oil, ashtrays, palettes and so on covered the entire surface of the table, filling the studio with a particularly evocative smell. The little patterned bowl has an inscription on its base, 'Mexico 1950'.*

Above *Music was always an element of studio life, 'Haydn or Mozart, never Wagner', according to Quentin. The androgynous nymph playing a lyre was painted on the gramophone cabinet by Angelica in 1936. Resting on the cabinet is a painting of Vanessa in front of her easel at La Souco, the home of Simon and Dorothy Bussy at Roquebrune in the south of France. Painted in 1960, it was probably the last of Duncan's many portraits of her. The mug, made by Phyllis Keyes and inscribed 'Monsieur' (Clive's sobriquet), was decorated in the 1930s by Vanessa.*

The studio is a treasure chest full of surprises - painted tiles, decorated furniture, pots and vases, fairground figures, academic casts, fabrics and screens, busts and family portraits. It takes first-time visitors several minutes to orientate themselves as they walk in, like adjusting to a sudden change of temperature, before they can focus on any one object or painting amid the heightened sensuality of the room.

The fireplace, with its tiled decorations and surround of amply proportioned naked youths, dominates. Duncan painted these figures in oil on plywood. The mantelshelf is pitted with holes from the innumerable drawing pins Duncan used to attach an assortment of ephemera - invitations, sketches, children's drawings, postcards, photographs, press-cuttings. The gleaming Pither stove flanked by armchairs invites one to sit down in comfort, listen to some music perhaps, or have a drink and a conversation.

Here, until World War Two, when Vanessa had a studio of her own constructed at the top of the house, Vanessa and Duncan worked together, happy and industrious, as Quentin described them, 'like two sturdy animals side by side in a manger, munching away contentedly, not needing to talk to each other but just happy in the presence of the other'.

Both the painters were dedicated to their work. Duncan had an almost religious belief in the activity of painting *per se*; he saw it as wholly virtuous. Never a day passed without him painting. At Charleston he might spend the morning in the studio. In the afternoon he might set off with his eccentric easel and paintbox piled into the back of his baby Austin to look for motifs. He would often bring his *plein air* sketches back to the studio to work on.

Cleaning up was not Duncan's strong point, and he was pretty ham-fisted at stretching canvases, so as often as not Vanessa did this for him. Duncan was catholic in his choice of materials. He liked charcoal, pen and ink, but happily used whatever came to hand. Often after dinner he would pick up an old envelope and begin sketching on it. Quentin said of Duncan's work: 'He [was] enormously serious about painting - he [was] as professional as a painter can be. There's a solidity, an organization about his best work which is also the work of a man who wants to live at peace with the world and to create that which is agreeable.'

Above Mixed Flowers, Charleston, c. *1932 by Vanessa. This exuberant still life was furnished by the garden and painted in the studio.*

Right *The oval gilt mirror replaces a rather larger one given to Duncan by Sickert and subsequently left by Duncan to a friend. To the right is shown the lower part of a pair of Italian fairground figures. Duncan, Clive, Vanessa and Roger Fry were all travelling in Italy in 1913 when Duncan set his heart on these figures being used to decorate a fairground stand. After some haggling Clive consented to buy a marvellously inexpensive 'Raphael' from the stallholder, and the figures were thrown in as part of the bargain. Duncan's easel stands in the foreground, with a pile of miscellaneous prints on the model's throne in front.*

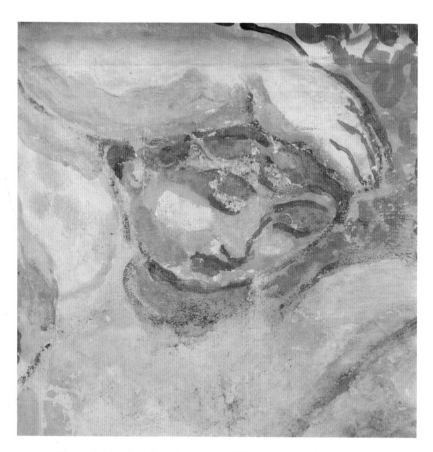

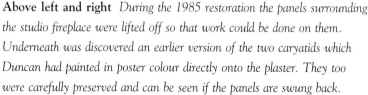

Above left and right *During the 1985 restoration the panels surrounding the studio fireplace were lifted off so that work could be done on them. Underneath was discovered an earlier version of the two caryatids which Duncan had painted in poster colour directly onto the plaster. They too were carefully preserved and can be seen if the panels are swung back.*

Opposite *The present panels around the fireplace were painted by Duncan around 1932. He also did the decorations above the mantelshelf in about 1925, while Vanessa designed the tiles behind the fireplace some time between 1925 and 1930. The figure on the mantelshelf is a cast of a sixth-century votive figure representing Kuan Yin, the ancient Chinese Goddess*

of Mercy. Roger Fry once owned the original, but before selling it he had two casts made, of which this is one. On the mantelpiece is Duncan's accumulation of photographs, invitation cards and pictures from newspapers and magazines which caught his eye. On the left is a glamorous studio photograph taken in the late 1930s of Angelica made up for a part in a play. A tile painted with a Turkish houri peers seductively over the top of a photograph of Queen Mary with two unidentified companions. The large framed photo-portrait is of Vanessa aged twenty-four; the stripy vase was picked up on some Mediterranean holiday, while the debonair 'film-star' in a hat is a studio photograph of Duncan taken in the 1930s. The military man is his father, Major Bartle Grant.

Left *Standing on the eighteenth-century Italian chest-of-drawers is Stephen Tomlin's original plaster bust of Virginia Woolf made in 1931, when she was forty-nine. 'I sat to Tommie … [he pinned] me there from 2 to 4 on 6 afternoons, to be looked at; & I felt like a piece of whalebone bent. This amused & interested me, at the same time I foamed with rage'* (*Diary, 7 August 1931*). *Virginia did not like being looked at, but Stephen Tomlin was very persuasive and somehow managed to get her to pose for her bust while she was sitting for Vanessa. But the work proceeded with difficulty and in the end it was left unfinished.*

To the left is a portrait of Adrian Stephen painted by Duncan in 1910, which shows the likeness between him and his sisters, Virginia and Vanessa. The youngest of the four Stephen children, he lived with them during the pre-World War One Bloomsbury period; it was a quarrelsome but fundamentally affectionate relationship. Adrian was to become one of the early Freudian psychoanalysts. To the right is a portrait of Duncan's mother, Ethel Grant, who did many of the embroideries in the house, painted in 1918. The little painted box is the work of Richard Shone, a friend of Duncan's who often visited Charleston in the later years. In the foreground is a clutch of ornaments made for necklaces by Quentin.

Above *Duncan's Self-portrait in a Turban was painted around 1909. Bloomsbury's passion for fancy dress underlay the famous 'Dreadnought Hoax' of 1910, when Duncan and a group of friends disguised in robes and turbans hoodwinked the Navy into believing they were Abyssinian dignitaries.*

Left *Duncan acquired this cast of the ears of Michelangelo's David from an art school in Lewes.*

However, Duncan was hopelessly generous when it came to selling his pictures. His good nature made him incapable of obtaining a realistic price for his work, and Quentin often described how poor Duncan let himself be exploited:

QB It was a desperate proceeding. He used to go round and mark on the back of his canvases £200. Then when somebody came as a serious purchaser he'd look at the back of the picture and see £200 and then would somehow feel it was impertinent to ask so much, so he'd say, 'Oh, well, no, no, I don't know, how about £150? Well that's a bit too much, say £100, well, £50, £25 perhaps.' He absolutely wasn't avaricious. I remember some boy - like so many of Duncan's boyfriends, semi-criminal - who had done a bunk with some money, together with some of Duncan's pictures, and Duncan had some nice American friends who were trying to help him get them back. Duncan was only concerned about the paintings: 'We must get those canvases back because they're not finished - about the money, nothing matters less after all.' So of course, Duncan was usually penniless.

There was an odd story of Duncan being invited to Roger Fry's house, Durbin's, but he never turned up, the reason being that he had kept five bob aside to pay for his journey but he had put it in such a secret place that he could not find it. And it was then that Roger thought that he must start something where painters could earn just a little money on the side: so he started the Omega Workshops.

Left *Reflected in the gilt mirror is the Dutch walnut glass-fronted cabinet which was one of a pair that once belonged to the novelist W.M. Thackeray; Vanessa inherited this piece of furniture from her father, whose first wife had been Thackeray's younger daughter Minnie. It contains antique glasses and decanters, and an eclectic range of ceramics, from Omega to Delft, some decorated by the Charleston artists, others acquired on their travels.*

Right above *In the late 1920s Duncan painted this design for the three-fold screen on paper, which was attached to the screen with drawing pins.*

Right *The small fireside table was painted by Vanessa around 1950.*

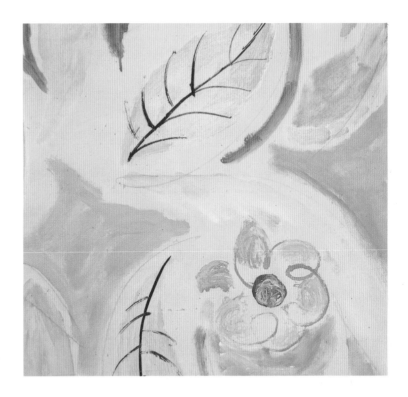

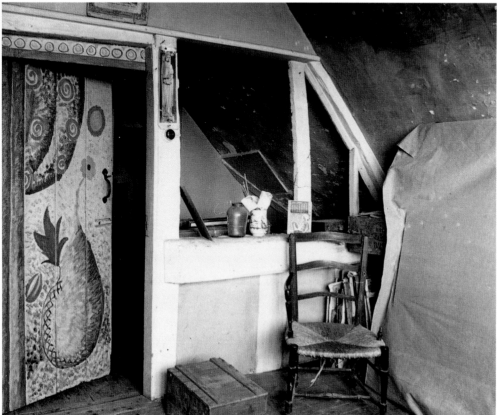

Left *Since her death, Vanessa's studio has been cleared; in the days when she used it the attic room was cluttered with the paraphernalia of a working painter and an enormous number of canvases was stored here. She also kept her sewing machine here, and a rag-bag of remnants, her photograph albums, and her collection of Virginia Woolf's books with jackets designed by her. The decorations on the door were done by Vanessa in 1939.*

Opposite *Self-portrait by Vanessa in her upstairs studio, 1952. Here, at the top of the house, Vanessa was, as Angelica described her, 'in heaven'. The view from the tall new window looked over the garden to the fields beyond and across to the distant Sussex Weald. Vanessa's grandchild Henrietta often sat for her portrait in the top studio and has described how well it suited her: 'I think that it is indicative of her character that . . . she worked at the top of the house. I believe that the view was essential to her. She needed light. She needed distant horizons. She was a woman with very clear views of her own. For Nessa could shock, astonish, leave one giddy with her point of view . . . Being with her, alone in the upper studio, was sometimes like looking at life from the height of a campanile tower.'*

In later years the studio doubled as a sitting room, especially in winter when it was the warmest room in the house. And avid performers as they were, the Charlestonians also used it for theatricals. It was possible to stretch a curtain across one end of the studio in such a way that the area in front of the door into 'Grant's Folly' became a convenient stage. Because the studio is L-shaped, the small branch of the L which leads into the walled garden could become hidden 'wings', serving for entry, exit and prompting, while the main part of the studio provided a comfortable auditorium. This division of the studio was used when the place was used for private theatricals. Having discovered a strange knack for writing any quantity of quite pointless dialogue, I produced one year a sketch which deserves to be recorded as a theatrical curiosity, in which members of the audience served as props.

The audience was asked to suppose that Charleston had for a long time been bereft of its original inhabitants. The performers took the roles of future visitors being conducted around the house by a guide. The audience was made to serve as properties. Thus when the guide pointed to Clive Bell, he was described as a writing desk which had served in previous ages for sentimental correspondence. Maynard Keynes was described as a safe, Leonard and Virginia Woolf were a pair of bookcases, and so on. It is strange now, when all that audience has gone, to remember that attempt to look into the future of Charleston.

A point came, in 1939, when the sociability of the studio drove Vanessa, who was in some ways a reclusive person, into hiding. It was decided that she should have a studio of her own. This was made at the top of the house in what had formerly been a spare bedroom. To do this it was necessary to construct a window facing north. It may sound hard on Vanessa that she had to walk up two flights of stairs every morning to work in what was in truth a very small room, but she saw the matter in another light. This was brought home to me at a time when the studio was very new.

It must have been soon after Maynard and Lydia arrived at Tilton. Lydia, in her well-meaning way, had just 'dropped in' with a party of guests to visit the Charlestonians, and in so doing had utterly wrecked a morning's work in the studio. They then left. Shortly afterwards, trying to find Vanessa for some banal reason,

I searched everywhere in vain until I discovered her in hiding with Duncan at the very top of the house. They feared that Lydia had made a return visit. Menaced by these social dangers, the artists were glad of an attic to which they could retire.

I think Vanessa at her best was an extraordinarily good painter. There was a kind of austerity and nobility about her work, and she also had a very happy decorative sense. Yet she always thought Duncan was a better painter than she. Perhaps in old age that was true, for she had a tendency then to go off into a kind of sentimental world of flowers and children. She loved her grandchildren too much, and it wasn't good for her painting.

VN Charleston is one of those adaptable houses which permits expansion, and for a family of artists nothing could be more natural than to turn chicken runs and attic bedrooms into

Above *During his time at the Staffordshire potteries, Quentin was taught to make stained glass by Gordon Forsyth, Principal of the Burslem Art School. 'A tiny window by me remains in what used to be my Charleston studio, and because I had the luck to get a few pieces of really lovely blue glass doesn't look too bad when the afternoon sun comes through it.'*

Opposite *Quentin designed the pottery in 1939; most of the ceramics and sculpture that he made for Charleston were thrown, modelled, fired and painted here. Recently renovated, it now has new shelves and a modern kiln and wheel, and is used by resident potters. A small bust by Quentin is visible here at the back of the shelf.*

studios. When, in the thirties, Quentin needed a space of his own in which to install a kiln and pottery wheel the obsolete wash house lent itself ideally to the purpose, though the room was haunted by fearful boyhood memories: 'The old wash house was a strange place, very bare and containing nothing save a pump and an enormous chimney breast beside which were a number of big coppers. One night I visited this place, it was dark and vaguely alarming. I went to the great chimney which led up to the open sky, but on this occasion it was blocked. I climbed up into it and encountered a man wearing a straw hat. "I am being eaten," he said. I looked, saw it was terribly true, and bolted screaming all the way back to my bed where very gradually I found that it had all been a dream. It was my worst nightmare and it was months before I could go alone into the wash house.'

The outer studio, as the wash house is now called, was nevertheless courageously appropriated by the adult Quentin and used to practise his newfound skills in ceramics and stained glass. Here he painted, potted, and pierced the wall with a small lustrous window which glows like a rainbow as the southern sunlight streams through it. Then in 1939, as war began to seem inevitable, Vanessa started to look at ways of rearranging the house as a permanent wartime retreat. This included converting the old chicken house into a pottery according to plans drawn up by Quentin. 'Work went on and gradually I got everything as I wanted it. But I knew that events were moving fast and on the day on which I used my new wheel for the first time Grace came in to say that the Germans were bombing Polish cities.'

For many years after the war, when Quentin was married and living far from Charleston in the north of England, he would return with his family, and work in the pottery during the holidays. Duncan and Vanessa loved to find a pristine set of cups and saucers newly fired and ready to be painted - rather to Quentin's chagrin, for he was looking forward to painting them himself!

In the 1950s the younger generation of Bells were banished to the outer studio, to avoid disrupting their grandparents at mealtimes. Our games often spread to the pottery, where we 'helped' Quentin with his pots. Sometimes we 'helped' Duncan and Vanessa by sitting to them for sixpence an hour.

Clive Bell's Bedroom

QB   I tend to think of Clive's bedroom as my bedroom, for it was here that my brother and I slept when we first came to the house in 1916. It was in this room that I remember performing an act, intended to imitate Charlie Chaplin, which consisted largely of filling my clothes with silver and crockery and then allowing it to escape from a hole in my immense pockets. Other high jinks produced a shower of plaster from the ceiling in the drawing room below. But my last distinct memory of sleeping, or of trying to sleep, in that room dates from just after the war, or more exactly from the summer of 1919. We boys had been in Scotland for three weeks with our Bell grandparents. When we returned we were met at the station by Clive and walked back to Charleston with him across the fields. It was a scorching hot day and after lunch I had so bad a headache that I retired to my bed to lie down. I remember lying there obsessed by odd, fantastic, waking dreams until at last I slept peacefully.

During the years of World War One Clive was an occasional visitor. His visits were, for us children, splendid occasions; he was usually accompanied by his mistress Mary Hutchinson and, what

The decorations in this room pre-date its ultimate occupant; they were carried out by Vanessa in 1917. She painted the beam running round the ceiling in a lemon yellow which, against the ochre of the walls, is somehow both discordant and subtly exhilarating. The charming little portrait of two children is curiously out of keeping with the majority of pictures in the house. It dates from about 1800 and is thought to show two young female ancestors of the Bell family. On the right of the bed is Quentin's copy (done before its sale in 1957) of Picasso's Pots et Citron, 1908. *Clive bought the original from the Paris dealer Kahnweiler in 1911; it was one of the earliest privately owned Picassos in England.*

for us was still more delightful, by chocolates. It has to be realized that then, with war shortages, chocolates were more usually dreamed of than eaten.

These visits by Clive were perhaps of psychological importance for me. In 1915 I had been part of a normal family with parents who lived together and with their children. By 1917 Clive was a rare visitor, while Duncan and Bunny were permanent residents. Clive spent the war at Garsington, the home of Lady Ottoline Morrell. The psychological strain should have been enormous, yet I was not aware of it. The part Clive played in my life was that of a generous and amusing figure, and though his appearances were rare, he was always entertaining.

I suppose he would have ranked as a rather poor father, but as I grew up he could be wonderfully sympathetic. I remember once after an exuberant party when, as happens when one is young on the morning after, I suffered from a moral hangover and felt deeply ashamed. I confessed to Clive that I was tortured by the memory of the utterly foolish things that I had said the night before. He smiled and said: 'Can you remember anything foolish that was said by any other guest?' I could not, and not only was I immediately comforted, but treasured the remark for the rest of my life.

In addition to that, I had a deep admiration for Clive in those days, because he seemed so splendidly and shamelessly successful. My father was a man of culture, a man of the world, a hedonist, a successful womanizer, a wonderful host and a wit. He was a man who loved to make other people happy, and who had several personae: the libertine, the hedonist, the sporting squire, but also the highbrow aesthete. He loved to go out after lunch with his dog and a gun, walking over the fields to return with a brace of pheasants. But he was also a man of letters and an intellectual,

Right *Vanessa painted* Charleston Pond *in 1919, from the window of what was later to be Clive's bedroom, but which was then her studio. An Omega vase stands on the sill. Another view of the pond (c. 1916) painted from here hangs in Duncan's studio downstairs.*

Opposite *Duncan decorated the corner cupboard when it was brought to Charleston in 1925. It is one of a pair, of which the other, undecorated, stands in Keynes's bedroom. To the right of it hangs a portrait of Angelica,* The Weaver, *painted by Vanessa in 1937. Angelica has many talents, and at various points in her life has been a weaver, painter, mosaicist, sculptor, patchwork-maker and writer. Clive brought the carpet to Charleston from 50 Gordon Square, London. It wore out, and this exact reproduction was woven specially by Avena Carpets in Halifax. The chair beneath Angelica's portrait is part of the set of six upholstered in the 'Grapes' fabric which Duncan designed for Allan Walton Ltd in 1932. The chintz curtains date from the 1950s.*

who loved a good argument and was perhaps happiest in conversation with his friends. He would have made the perfect eighteenth-century gentleman. He seemed to be all the things that I was not but that I still hoped that I might be. It was not perhaps a great ideal to pursue, but at that time I pursued it in a spirit of passionate admiration.

In 1939, when the Charlestonians prepared to face the rigours of war, Clive brought his furniture and other belongings from 50 Gordon Square, where until then he had lived a very social life - being, to all intents and purposes, a bachelor. His arrival at Charleston gave the place an unusual degree of respectability, what he would have called *tenue*. But it also created tensions.

Clive had always complained that when he was in Sussex he was very ill accommodated; Vanessa decided to put an end to this fancied grievance and the whole of the north end of the upstairs part of the house was refurbished and put at his disposal. He was provided with, in effect, a self-contained flat, his bedroom being made to communicate with the bathroom and the library. Nevertheless, he still managed to be petulant about his accommodation. Virginia Woolf wrote : 'Clive at Charleston yesterday . . . A little testy about his room. I needn't say I've been palmed off with the worst in [the] house. Desiring sympathy, Duncan said, & admiration. All his books were put in order by the others' (Virginia Woolf *Diary*, 7 August 1939).

Above *The unusual reading stand is mahogany and dates from the mid-nineteenth century. On it is an exhibition catalogue from 1949, 'Balzac à Vendome'. Clive read French fluently and voraciously, although his spoken French was imperfect.*

Opposite *The books include paperbound volumes of works by Sainte-Beuve, Prosper Mérimée and Roger Martin du Gard. The pictures above the bookcase are, from left to right:* Landscape, *c. 1920-22, by Othon Friesz, inscribed to Clive Bell 'en toute sympathie' by the artist;* Pear and Apple, *c. 1920, also by Othon Friesz;* Fairy Pipe, *c. 1925-28, by Pierre Roy;* Three Fish on a Plate, *early 1920s, probably by Edouard Richard, a French painter who had been praised by Clive for a recent exhibition in Paris in an article in Vogue in 1925, and* Still Life of Fruit, *c. 1922-24, by Henri Hayden, inscribed to Clive Bell. The armchair is upholstered in a Laura Ashley reproduction of Vanessa's original 'White' fabric, which she designed for the Omega Workshops in 1913.*

Yet Clive made his bedroom very much his own. There was a large easy chair for him to sit in and read his French novels, and he even brought his own carpet from London - it is the only fitted carpet in the house. He adorned the south wall with a line of paintings which were mostly presents to him from French artists whom he visited in their studios. Not a wildly exciting galaxy of painters. Perhaps the most sympathetic is Pierre Roy who was known in Paris as 'le grand père du surréalisme'.

The decorated bed in this room lays perhaps the most obvious claim to our attention, and perhaps to ribald comment. Provided originally to accommodate Clive's *vie amoureuse* in the 1920s and a notable feature of his flat in 50 Gordon Square, it also made a number of other sentimental journeys, ending in the possession of his last mistress Barbara Bagenal, who very handsomely returned it to Charleston.

VN Clive's relationship with Barbara Bagenal was the last of his 'sentimental adventures'. A vivacious, willing, carefree character, Barbara could nevertheless be maddeningly intrusive, so it came as rather a shock to the other inhabitants of Charleston when Clive took up with her in his old age. But, almost as a matter of principle, Clive felt he ought to be provided with female company, so he endured the teasing and the laughter in return for the kind of cosseting that only Barbara could offer. Quentin wrote: 'She could see that he was well-dressed and well-fed, taken to his club and fetched back again, chauffeured, doctored, reassured and provided with an opportunity every day to write a few lines of well-tailored English prose. Barbara could manage it all. Clive, for his part, had something to offer in return.'

All his life Clive was an ardent Francophile, a love he passed on to his son. Although his spoken French was never really very good (Quentin's was much more fluent) his vocabulary was tremendous and he experienced intense enjoyment simply from being on the other side of the Channel. When Quentin was a young man Clive and he were together in Paris. 'That was one of the few occasions on which I have seen him put out - we were seated in some kind of café-concert and it became obvious from the comments of the other members of the public there that they believed Clive to be my lover and I his faggot!'

As the erotic nude line drawing by Segonzac above the bed is no doubt intended to suggest, Clive was anything but homosexual. Most of his life he was a great flirt with an eye for a pretty face. But in later years his taste in women faltered. By then Quentin had become more critical of his father's undiscerning susceptibility, and he described the unfortunate effect of the breakdown of his relationship with Mary Hutchinson: 'One symptom of his troubles was a kind of desperate womanizing; indignant ladies had to struggle to escape from passionate advances which they had never encouraged.' There was also an intense romantic correspondence which he carried on with a young woman who was a *vendeuse* in a big Parisian shop; for a while he could talk of nothing else but this *amour*. Quentin then fortuitously found himself in a restaurant in Paris and ran into Clive and the young lady having lunch together. 'She was quite hideous,' he later recalled.

Clive was not particularly vain about his appearance; however, he always had trouble with his hair. He began to grow bald early, and attempted to cover the dome of his head with several long strands combed from one side to the other. Given an upward draught from an electric fan it could stand on end. 'Most unfortunate', as Quentin described it.

QB I once asked Vanessa whether Clive had been a very handsome young man when she married him. 'No,' she said, 'but he was very amusing.' I think that although she felt that he became very worldly, and could be very silly about his girlfriends, still he could make her laugh and in later years there was something of an echo of past fun in her manner towards him. For some reason there was one gesture, Vanessa stretching out her arms towards him as she passed a plate of salt beef, which reminded me of that distant time when they had been in love and in lust. It was a tiny domestic gesture which never failed to move me. And although there was plenty of teasing, I never heard a harsh or cruel word exchanged between those models of conjugal infidelity. Neither did I ever see a passionate embrace between them.

Ours was an elastic home, it never broke. Clive, Duncan and Vanessa lived on good terms and it is to the credit of both my parents that they remained amicable for the fifty years or so of their married lives.

Above *This photograph of Clive was probably taken at his pied-à-terre, 50 Gordon Square, in 1922. Clive liked to be correctly dressed, whether in the city or at Charleston. Pipe in hand, he appears solidly dignified.*

Opposite *The curious panel next to the bed dates from 1917; it is part of the decorative scheme carried out by Vanessa when the room was her studio. A photograph from that time shows the bands of red and grey, but the Italian hand-printed papers were added later. Vanessa painted the head and end boards of Clive's eighteenth-century French provincial bed in about 1950. She probably also decorated the three-legged sexagonal bedside table around 1920. Over the bed-head is* Female Nude, *a pen and ink drawing of c. 1924 by André Dunoyer de Segonzac.*

The Green Bathroom

VN Beauty was important to the Charlestonians, but so were comfort and cleanliness, where they could be afforded. When they first arrived in 1916, there was a lavatory and bathroom, but the bath had only cold water. That state of affairs persisted until the end of World War One. Quentin describes it thus: 'There was the bathless period 1916-1919, the bath period 1919-1939, and the multi-bath period from 1939.'

In winter the bathless period involved submitting to bathing in a hip-bath before the dining room fire. The bath period was not much better, although there was hot water. As Quentin said, 'the only bathroom in the house (it is a bleak and unglamorous affair) was that which is situated at the foot of the stairs which lead up to Vanessa's studio'. Frances Partridge survived the ordeal of the early 'bath period' with equanimity: 'In winter you might suffer severely from the cold, and at the time of my first visit there in the mid nineteen-twenties there was only one bathroom containing a narrow bath short of enamel and giving out a hollow tinny sound, whose pipes dripped gently but steadily, in

This bathroom was originally known as the green room; green paint appears to have been used lavishly around the house during the early period 1916-18, to cover wallpapers and paintwork, as traces of similar paint were discovered in a number of other rooms in the house during the restoration. By 1970, when Duncan Grant's friend, Richard Shone, painted this nude decoration on the bath panel, the bathroom had been re-painted in cream. Richard now says he perhaps would not have chosen these colours against a green background had he known the room was to have been restored to its original colour. However, the overall effect does have a certain brilliance and dash. The picture over the bath is Apples *by Duncan, c. 1935-40.*

spite of being wrapped in yellowing newspapers. Yet hot baths were there for everyone who wanted them, and brass cans were brought to all the bedrooms.'

By 1926, with the security of a long lease, Vanessa felt able to take steps to improve conditions. Radiators were installed, the tinny bath was re-enamelled, and the hot water system upgraded. Julian and Quentin, the ungrateful editors of the *Charleston Bulletin* (their handwritten daily newspaper), were critical of the new arrangements:

'On first entering the house one is struck by the overwhelming odour of paint, emanating from the new radiators. On first entering the bath one sticks to the bottom and turns white in patches owing to the imperfectly dried Chinese white congealed at the bottom. The old square hot water tank, so useful for drying clothes on, has been replaced by an obese cylender [sic] crowned with an abrupt cone on which no garment will remain.'

The multi-bath era commenced in 1939 with the installation of both Vanessa's bath in her own bedroom and Clive's independent bathroom. Quentin recalled: 'Until then Clive's bathroom was a place for storing pictures. With the library and his

bedroom, the addition of a bathroom made Clive's area of the house as self-contained, comfortable and independent as was possible under the circumstances.'

From a reclining position, immersed in hot water, Clive could enjoy one of the best views from any bath in Sussex, over the walled garden and out to the meadows and weald beyond. In her autobiography, *Deceived with Kindness*, Angelica has provided a vivid picture of Clive's morning ablutions:

'A bad sleeper but of regular, predictable habits, Clive took time, after Grace had brought his jug of hot water and had drawn his curtains, to wash and dress. Unlike Vanessa's, his toilet was a semi-public affair, and he could be heard shuffling on his carpeted floor from bathroom to bedroom . . . blowing his nose, gargling, brushing his teeth and talking to himself, while a delicate smell of toilet water seeped under the door and one could imagine him stretching out his chin to meet the razor. Finally, pink as a peach, perfumed and manicured but in old darned clothes of once superlative quality, he would enter the room and tap the barometer, the real function of which was to recall his well-ordered Victorian childhood. After greeting Vanessa he would help himself to coffee and settle down with deliberation to eat an orange, dry toast and marmalade.'

An orderly person, Clive pinned a small list to the wall above the linen basket in the corner of the bathroom. Every time he put something in - handkerchief, shirt, or underwear - he made a note of it, so that he could check on its return from the laundry.

The rest of the household and guests were mainly left to use the 'bleak and unglamorous' remaining bathroom, in which Grace too was allowed to bath once a week, on Tuesday afternoons.

Left *On the shelf by the mirror is* Flowers in a Jug, *c. 1930-35 by Keith Baynes. The small table was decorated by Duncan in the 1930s.*

Opposite *In 1970, when Duncan was too decrepit to lie on the floor painting baths, he delegated the task to his friend Richard Shone. Richard based the voluptuous lady on a drawing by Delacroix he had found reproduced in a book at Charleston.*

The Library

QB The Library is a large, square room with two windows. The one facing west used to have a prospect of the fields towards Firle until the construction of the studio interrupted it; the other looking north commands the view of the walled garden and the weald beyond. This room was for some years Vanessa's bedroom, and although she moved out of it in 1939 when it became Clive's library, her presence, in the form of a regal portrait by Duncan, still dominates the room.

The eighteenth-century style of the Venetian chairs, the stately and serious impression that is always produced by an orderly collection of volumes, tell one much about Clive's tastes and preferences. This impression is not contradicted, rather it is reinforced by the thoroughly Post-Impressionist manner in which the door panels have been painted, by the copy (made by Roger Fry in about 1917) of an early Italian master, and by Duncan Grant's slightly frivolous painted cupboard doors on the large bookcase.

In due course books completely filled every wall of the library, on bookcases of makeshift shelving. They contained a heterogeneous collection, ranging from long and heavy works in Greek with Latin footnotes (relics of Clive's Cambridge years), Dodsley's eighteenth-century plays, Walpole's letters, Boswell, Johnson, Pepys, Byron and Thackeray, to every cheap novel that Clive ever purchased at a bookstall in the Gare St Lazare to while away a day's travel. This was not the only room Clive used for reading and writing; for many years he worked in the ground-floor study, which is very close to the most socially active part of the house. But in the end he found that this position was, as he would have put it, altogether too *mouvementé*, i.e. noisy, and he then resorted more frequently to the library upstairs.

During the restoration, the makeshift shelving on the south wall was removed to allow more space for hanging pictures, but despite the reduction in the number of books the room still contains everything that Proust, Maupassant, Mme de Sévigné and St Simon ever wrote.

VN By comparison with some of the rooms at Charleston, the library has an atmosphere of austerity which is somehow appropriate. The sombre black walls, accentuated with vertical bands of Venetian red in the corners, have been there since the early days. The idea of having plain walls highlighted with contrasting colours was one which had originally impressed Vanessa in 1901 when she visited the Surrey home of Charles Furse who was painting her portrait. But at Charleston, black is never just black, and white is never just white. Angelica Garnett helped with the restoration of the house. She has an acute memory for colour and was tormented by the difficulty of reproducing the exact shade of black she remembered from her childhood. The elusive effect she sought could only be recaptured by roundabout means. 'Eventually I realized,' she wrote, 'that the black was influenced by the minute green leaves of the wallpaper it had been painted over . . . and in the end I had to be content with mixing in a fraction of yellow which I put on in two coats and, as it then looked too solid, vigorously scrubbed off again with a yard broom.'

The large bookcase came from Clive's London flat and was decorated for him by Duncan in about 1925 with voluptuous mandolin players on the cupboard doors. The books include works by Cervantes, St Simon, Balzac, Swift, Walpole and Byron. The Venetian chairs are part of Clive's set of six upholstered in Duncan's 'Grapes' fabric. On the table is a copy of L'Amour de l'Art *from the 1920s and a ceramic bowl decorated by Duncan. A Foley vase made by Quentin in 1938 stands on the shelf.*

Above *'I keep thinking of the many times when one could talk to Lytton and he seemed to see further into things than anyone else could,' Vanessa wrote after Lytton Strachey's death in 1932. Stephen Tomlin's bronze bust of Lytton was done two years earlier at Ham Spray, the house Lytton shared with the artist Dora Carrington and her husband Ralph Partridge, and belonged to the sitter. On the shelf beside him is a Staffordshire figure. Clive was a great admirer of Lytton Strachey as a writer and although Tomlin's head of him did not stand on the windowsill in his day, its current position seems appropriate.*

Right *The north-facing window shown here in the late afternoon light gives a lovely view over the walled garden and the fields beyond. In 1917, when this was Vanessa's bedroom, Duncan painted Henry, the family's lurcher, below the window and the cockerel above it 'to guard her at night and wake her up in the morning'. The dog's benign appearance is deceptive; not long after the family moved to Charleston, Henry had to be sent away for terrorizing the servants. The curtains are chintz, and were probably bought by Vanessa in the 1920s.*

Above The Entry into Jerusalem *by Frederick Etchells. Duncan bought the painting soon after it had been exhibited by Etchells in Paris in 1912; its frame was also decorated by the artist.*

Left *Duncan painted the Gainsborough-esque portrait of Vanessa in his downstairs studio in 1942. To the left of the portrait hangs Roger Fry's copy of one of the frescoes in the Upper Church, San Francesco, Assisi, showing 'The Healing of the Wounded Man of Lerida', by the Master of the St Cecilia Altarpiece. It was shown in an exhibition of copies at the Omega Workshops in 1917.*

Opposite *There are further echoes of the early Renaissance in the figures on the door panels, whose headgear is reminiscent of some of Piero della Francesca's Arezzo frescoes. Painted by Duncan in 1917-18, their angular forms are in emphatic contrast to his later curvaceous musicians on the bookcase cupboard doors.*

Maynard Keynes's Bedroom

VN   Duncan and Vanessa's friendship with Maynard Keynes went back to the early days of Bloomsbury and its origins in Cambridge at the turn of the century. His love affair with Duncan ended in 1909, but their friendship remained strong and Maynard was an important figure in both Duncan's and Vanessa's lives, not least financially. His sympathies were those of a man of culture and taste, but it was his job at the Treasury and his insider's understanding of politics that made him unique in Bloomsbury.

Maynard gradually became part of the Charleston *ménage* during the years of World War One and the early twenties. As their most frequent guest he was allocated his own bedroom. The room is unusual in having entirely white, undecorated walls; in a fit of purity, Vanessa purged the room in 1947, when it had become Quentin's. 'You can't imagine what a whited palace this is becoming,' she wrote to Angelica. 'The whole of Quentin's library and other possessions have been turned upside down and his room made snow white and pearl grey . . . I expect he won't notice. Still it really is a change for the better' (Vanessa to Angelica Garnett, 14 September 1947). Nevertheless the room contains some colourful early painted furniture by Duncan. The bed, presided over by a rather sinister head of Morpheus, is probably the most notable object. The paintings include a likeness of Bunny

Another of Quentin's experiments with the medium of stained glass is in the upper door panel of Keynes's bedroom, although by the time it was installed (in about 1940) Keynes had long removed to nearby Tilton House and the room was Quentin's own. Over the bed hangs Duncan's Bathers by the Pond, c. 1921. *'Duncan is painting a picture of 2 nudes by a pond rather under the influence of Seurat I think - very odd pale relief' (Vanessa to Roger Fry, 21 August 1921).*

Garnett by Duncan, and a portrait of Julian who at one time occupied this room. When the room became Quentin's, he created its only fixed decorative feature - the stained-glass panel in the door which leads out onto the head of the staircase.

QB   One cloudy and sunny day when I was a child, I ascended the stairs from the hall and noticed a ray of light which escaped through the keyhole of the Keynes room door. This tiny ray widened and fell upon the blank white wall opposite as though upon a cinema screen and, as in the cinema, an image appeared, upside-down - at first very indistinct and then, as the clouds lifted out of doors, lovely, bright and distinct with a wealth of detail. I saw the window bars, the foliage of the willow tree on the other side of the pond, and a projected view of the entire countryside looking towards Tilton. It was enchanting, and the thought struck me that, with pencil and paper the scene might be captured, but here my hand failed me. I did however think that I had made a remarkable discovery, until I was taken to Eastbourne and shown the *camera obscura* on the pier. The way in which the light fell that day must have been pure chance, for I cannot recall ever seeing that lovely image again.

The room overlooks the pond at the front of the house, and in summer its window was smothered in the flowers of a splendid white clematis which covered the façade. Dorothy Bussy, a friend of Gide and Matisse, declared, when visiting the house, that all that was needed to complete the scene was a large blonde in a negligée to look out of the window. But this was never supplied.

Almost every weekend during World War One would find a new copy of the *Evening Standard* on the shelf outside the kitchen where lamps and candles stood. This meant that Maynard was in the house. With his black Treasury bag there was something faintly

Above *Duncan painted this portrait of Maynard Keynes working on his* Treatise on Probability *when the two were on holiday together in the Orkneys in 1908.*

Opposite *The bookcase, painted by Quentin in the 1960s, contains file boxes decorated by Quentin and his family to contain copies of documents used for his biography of Virginia Woolf, written 1967-72. The terracotta figurines on the shelf are by Quentin; on the left 'Europe'; on the right 'Fashions of 1860'. Quentin was an avid historian (though in no sense a follower) of fashion, and his first book was a treatise on the theory of fashion,* On Human Finery *(1947). The paintings are, from the left:* The Duomo, Lucca, *1949, by Vanessa,* Portrait of David Garnett, *c. 1915, by Duncan. 'Bunny' Garnett was twenty-three when this was painted; he lived at Charleston during World War One and in 1942 married Angelica. On the right is* Brighton Pier, *c. 1955, by Vanessa.*

suspicious about his appearance and we boys perpetuated the myth that he (like Lytton Strachey with his redoubtable beard) was actually a spy. The reality was that we were never in any doubt of his being our friend.

VN One weekend his luggage contained something even more momentous than his Treasury papers. Maynard had been to Paris during the 1918 bombardment by the Germans to attend the sale of Degas's collection of pictures. He had persuaded the wartime Chancellor that the timing of the sale was propitious for acquiring masterpieces for the nation, and was allowed 550,000 francs to spend.

Although he bought a Delacroix, a Corot, four Ingres and two Manets, Maynard could not persuade the Director of the National Gallery to bid for a Cézanne, so bought it for himself. When he returned to England he was so overloaded with luggage that he had to deposit some of it in the hedge at the bottom of the Charleston lane. Vanessa wrote to Roger Fry: 'We had great excitements about the pictures. Maynard came back suddenly and unexpectedly late at night, having been dropped at the bottom of the lane . . . and said he had left a Cézanne by the roadside! Duncan rushed off to get it . . . and it's most exciting to have it in the house' (Vanessa to Roger Fry, 3 April 1918).

Maynard's purchase of the Cézanne typically combined shrewdness and opportunism, and part of the thrill for his friends came from seeing him in a position of power at a time of international drama. As Quentin has written, 'There was something immensely exciting about his involvement with the conflict.'

QB Maynard was happily confident about a victorious outcome to the war, indeed his optimism seemed to border on hubris; perhaps that is a little severe, but Maynard was informed, as he came from the very seat of power. He was the only member of Bloomsbury to hold a position of importance in the wartime governments and when he said that we were winning and that victory would soon be ours we believed him and went on believing him until his promise was fulfilled.

After the armistice was declared, Maynard divided his time between Charleston and France where he worked on drawing up the Versailles Peace Treaty of 1919. He seemed to be continually

Above *Both the plates beside the window were made by Quentin in the 1940s. Janie Bussy decorated the one above, and he the one below.*

Opposite *The linen chest was painted by Duncan in about 1917. Inside the lid is a mythological scene humorously entitled 'Leda and the Duck'; he did several versions of this motif whose title was a gentle send-up of 'Leda and the Swan' of Greek legend. In the window is a rush-seated Sussex settle of about 1850, a gift from Mary Hutchinson to Clive.*

travelling, and his visits were always fascinating as he described the intrigues and follies of Versailles.

Finally he could no longer endure the diplomats and their diplomacies; he resigned from the Treasury and settled more or less permanently at Charleston, occupying this bedroom, where he wrote his famous denunciation of the Peace Treaty, *The Economic Consequences of the Peace*.

Maynard's strong-minded approach to life extended to his domination of the Charleston household. He insisted on instituting 'Charleston Time', which was one hour ahead of British Summer Time; this did not go down well with Clive and played havoc with the kitchen staff whose routine was in tatters. Yet he became and remained one of my favourite grown-ups, always ready to explain his activities and ideas in terms that a child could understand and, as it now seems to me, very patient. His marriage to Lydia in 1925 brought to an end Maynard's tenancy at Charleston; he abandoned at the same time the last of his boyfriends, that amiable philosopher Jack Sprott, and the Keyneses then established themselves a few hundred yards away at Tilton.

But Lydia, it must be said, did not altogether please my elders and betters, and it was not without difficulty that they could accept Mrs Maynard Keynes as a close neighbour. Vanessa's friendship with Maynard had a special value for her, and although they were not lovers, there had always been an unusual degree of intimacy between them, using that term in its correct sense. And now ruthlessly, though without any unkind intentions, Maynard was bringing that relationship to an end; a younger woman had taken her place and all the old fun and games between them were at an end. Duncan must have had something of the same feeling of exclusion. Clive complicated matters further, for he had a kind of standing flirtation with Lydia, which Maynard very naturally resented.

However, for me it was a natural and in no way a distressing thing when Lydia and Maynard got married. Although in later years I began to understand why the Charlestonians sometimes found it difficult to endure Lydia's company - for let me be frank, there were times when Lydia could have bored for Russia - I never ceased to find her deeply sympathetic.

Right *Duncan painted the bedhead for Vanessa in about 1917. It depicts Morpheus, god of sleep, described by the Latin poet Ovid as 'sending dreams and visions of human forms' to the sleeper. The god's wooden nose stands out in sharp relief from the headboard and makes one wonder whether repose in this bed would have been possible. Vanessa's initials are painted on the reverse side of the headboard.*

Left *The firescreen, decorated by Duncan in the 1930s, is formed by two movable panels. It was probably done for the annual sale of the London Artists' Association, and not having found a buyer returned to Charleston. Above it hangs Charleston, Vanessa's only known painting of the front of the house, done in about 1950. The figure of Clive can be seen strolling across the terrace. The plates on either side were made by Quentin, but Duncan decorated the one on the left and Vanessa the one on the right. Quentin also made the figurines on the mantelpiece.*

Right *The lilypond table was designed by Duncan in 1913-14, based on an oil sketch he had made of the goldfish pond in Roger Fry's garden at Durbins. The design was adapted to a number of screens and table tops, and proved to be one of the Omega Workshops' most popular products. The table has legs that fold flat under the base; as a result it is somewhat rickety. The rag rug was made to a traditional design by an old lady who lived in nearby Ringmer and was an acquaintance of Grace Higgens.*

Duncan Grant's Bedroom

QB In the autumn of 1935 I found myself alone at Charleston - the rest of the family having gone to Paris, Shanghai, Liverpool and other unlikely places. I remained developing a sore throat and a high temperature. Luckily Grace was there to look after me. Having been away for a year, I had no room that I could fairly claim; I therefore retired to Duncan's bedroom with six half-bottles of wine presented to me by Maynard. I have rarely felt more comfortable anywhere than I was then, and although I had duties that called me I was reluctant to respond to them. I have slept in all the bedrooms at Charleston but this is my favourite. To my mind Duncan's bedroom has the most complete decorative scheme of any in the house.

Coming into this room always reminds me of Christmas morning 1918. Christmas Eve had, as always, been a time of excitement and speculation. As usual we boys had had some difficulty in going to sleep and we were downstairs in what is now called Clive's study. We became aware of something unusual happening and I had a momentary glimpse of a stranger in the hall.

Then in the morning came the presents, and I found to my delight that Julian had given me a gun, the hammer of which exploded a percussion cap. It was a moment of great joy. But there was another gift, not quite so exciting but yet momentous. Upstairs in Duncan's bedroom, lying in the bed where it stands now, was Vanessa with an absurdly small creature, very pink and strange, which I touched very gently with one finger - my sister.

VN The children grew up unaware of Angelica's parentage. Nominally, Clive Bell was her father, and yet her features and her very existence were testimony to Vanessa's lifelong passion for the homosexual Duncan. This was a relationship which Vanessa never thought necessary to discuss with her children. In her upbringing of them she left them free to draw their own conclusions, but also to some extent free from guidance. But Quentin was aware that their household was not like other people's - 'I think I was worried by our lack of respectability' - and there were occasions when he realized that what took place behind closed doors at Charleston and in Bloomsbury was unorthodox.

QB We were never told that there was anything in which we ought to believe or disbelieve apart from what one may call domestic morality: 'be kind to each other and don't be a nuisance'. I can remember no kind of propaganda that was put our way. In so far as we received guidance, it was teaching by example: we saw how our parents behaved, how they discussed things and how they managed their lives; we laughed at them and with them.

I did see Vanessa in Duncan's arms once. I was coming into that room at Charleston which is now called Duncan's bedroom. It was dark; I held a candle, and I saw them through the open door. I at once dropped my candle . . . tactful little boy? No, just clumsy. Presumably they had no light, for the room was for a few minutes quite dark. By the time light had been restored any little embarrassment was over and there were other things that had to be discussed. I cannot associate this memory with any very strong emotion. But I do remember that Duncan seemed to have grown taller and Vanessa shorter; she was stretching up to kiss him on tiptoe, and yet I always thought of them as being of equal height.

The room has a view east over the pond. The window seat is French, c. 1830, its cover was designed by Vanessa in 1943 and worked by Ethel Grant. Vanessa painted the decorations in the window embrasure 1925-30. On the sill stands a nineteenth-century bronze figurine after the antique of Narcissus, and a plaster cast of a Benin head from the British Museum.

VN Quentin knew Duncan all his life, and yet he told me that, in a way, he always felt he never knew him properly. 'He was certainly not a father-figure to me - more of an elder brother. As Angelica's father he was non-committal and really rather limited. Although he cared for her, I don't think he cared for the whole situation very much. There was this secret side to his life which he didn't want to show to me.'

Quentin was referring to Duncan's love affairs with men; these were numerous and included liaisons with close Bloomsbury friends such as Bunny Garnett, Maynard Keynes, Adrian Stephen and Lytton Strachey, as well as a disparate range of homosexual policemen, prisoners, artists' models, poets and painters, some more serious than others. These passions were at times the source of grief and anger to Vanessa, and even Clive could be indignant on her behalf when he saw how Duncan's behaviour upset her. Duncan's sympathies were too easily aroused; they may have seemed selfish, yet they combined sensuality with real affection, and over time Vanessa became resigned to his incapacity for total commitment. Their sexual relationship ended with Angelica's birth. To Roger Fry, Vanessa wrote, 'I am nearly always very happy with Duncan . . . He likes being with me enough for me to be quite happy, and as you say it is so much to be able to lead this kind of life.' But between concealing her child's parentage, and keeping up appearances in public on the one hand while on the other spending as much time as she could with the man she loved, Vanessa had to achieve a difficult balancing act.

The door opening into Duncan's bedroom shows the ceramic number plate betraying Charleston's previous identity as a summer guest-house. The ornate nineteenth-century prie-dieu chair is decorated with beadwork - not good for kneeling on, one might think - indeed some people have doubted whether this was its function. It is one of a pair, made in Dublin and bought by Duncan in Brighton in 1918. When he saw them, Clive is reported to have exclaimed with horror, 'Now, Duncan, you have gone too far!' Above it hangs Vanessa's portrait of Angelica, painted in 1930 when she was twelve. The head of Vanessa on the early-nineteenth-century French provincial chest-of-drawers is by Marcel Gimond, and was made in 1920-21. Gimond also did the red chalk sketch hanging beside it.

Yet very few people who met Duncan remained immune to his charm, which lay in his natural unselfconsciousness. 'He could take unbelievable liberties . . . Once for a bet Duncan walked dressed only in a blanket from Fitzroy Square to Gordon Square and got away with it.' For Angelica there was always a quality of mystery about her father's character: 'He may have and often did tease people, but he did not walk naked under a blanket to prove that he had a sense of humour. This I feel certain of though I cannot tell you why he did it! It was this mystery that gave his acts their fascination; he was by no means a "professional charmer", but a man of instinct, and this was what made him so different from the rest of Bloomsbury.'

Clothed, Duncan had a reputation for a kind of casual panache: 'he could, on occasion, get himself up quite pretty'. For painting, however, he put on more or less whatever came to hand - a palimpsest of shirts, waistcoats and pullovers in no particular order. Virginia Woolf described him as 'incredibly wrapped round with yellow waistcoats, spotted ties, and old blue stained painting jackets. His trousers have to be hitched up constantly.' 'His dress could be so appalling,' said Quentin, 'that one time Ottoline Morrell came and complained to me and said, "It's not proper, Duncan wearing those things."'

Both Quentin and Angelica have commented on Duncan's gift for sleep - how he could curl up like a hedgehog and drop off in any adverse circumstances at any time of day. He could nap in the back of a broken-down car while mechanics worked around him repairing it. At Charleston he often carried on sleeping long after the family had assembled for breakfast. When this happened Angelica either struck up an irritating little Beethoven *Ecossaise* on the piano directly below his room, or went to rouse him herself. She would find him snoozing peacefully in bed, the room full of the scent of the apples and pears which he often left to ripen on the windowsill.

Eventually, in extreme old age, Duncan relinquished this room and moved downstairs to sleep in what had been Vanessa's bedroom, next to the studio. Marcel Gimond's head of Vanessa remains in its place on the chest-of-drawers here, a memorial to nearly fifty years of shared life.

Below and opposite *Vanessa enclosed a sketch of her symmetrical design for Duncan's room in a letter she wrote to Roger Fry while she was painting it. 'I've been painting that old still life of apples in the dish every day lately and also painting the two doors in Duncan's bedroom. They come on either side of the mantelpiece you know which makes it rather an amusing whole but I'm not doing anything very startling - only pots of flowers and marbled circles' (Vanessa to Roger Fry, 22 February 1917).*

The colours of these decorations are enhanced by their juxtaposition with the expanses of plain white walls in the room; these are painted not in that dead, flat, clean white beloved of laboratories and catering institutions, but in a subtle white distemper containing both black and burnt sienna. Above the mantelpiece is Vanessa's 1922 copy of Raphael's St Catherine; the original is in the National Gallery in London.

Left above *Duncan's dressing room can be glimpsed through the door. Over the large mirror is a copy of Vanessa's boldly composed, Omega-influenced Tea Things, 1919. The large square stool has its seat upholstered with cross-stitched canvas worked by Duncan's mother to his design in 1924-25.*

Left *Duncan in 1933, seated on a table outside the garden room.*

Left *The dressing room overlooks the farm buildings; beyond them rises the summit of Firle beacon. The small table in front of the window was decorated by Duncan around 1945 with a spirited depiction of Arion astride a rather unconvincing dolphin. Herodotus recounts how, in Greek myth, the poet Arion was condemned to die by the sailors whose ship was carrying him home. He leapt overboard and was rescued by a dolphin. Duncan's sketch of a horse is undated.*

Above *The fact that Duncan had a dressing room might seem curious in view of his sartorial casualness. He also kept his family pictures and books here. His reading matter ranged from Tolstoy and Walter Pater to Gracie Fields and Cecil Beaton. The silhouettes, copies by Duncan of the much smaller originals taken in 1831, were also mounted by him. They represent Duncan's Plowden ancestors from his mother's side; left to right, Henrietta Plowden, Sophia Plowden and Mr Plowden their father.*

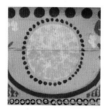

The Spare Bedroom

QB   In the early days at Charleston, we boys were shifted about a good deal, and what is now called the spare room was one of our numerous night nurseries. I still always think of it as 'our bedroom', and perhaps this was our favourite, for in a cold house it was usually warm, being situated above the kitchen.

My brother slept to the left of the window, I to the right. It was in this room that Julian kept his museum, a grisly collection of the heads of birds shot with an airgun and, in some primitive and inefficient way, preserved. It was also our editorial office - for it was here that the *Charleston Bulletin* was composed and typed.

In the twenties Charleston had its own newspaper, a periodical which consciously imitated the early efforts at journalism of my Aunt Virginia and her siblings. They as children had collaborated in writing a weekly newspaper called *The Hyde Park Gate News*. But the *Charleston Bulletin* was a daily and the effort involved in producing it was really too great - for some. Julian got bored with it, the two of us disagreed, and for a long time the younger journalist was left to carry the editorial burden single-handed. As Editor I rose at 5.30 am to get it written and delivered at breakfast - not the habit of a lazy child! Like so many people I could work very hard so long as the work was called play. The 'grown-ups' were of course encouraging with their praise of it: 'The Bulletin has been very much to the fore lately. Large numbers appear every day and its journalese is becoming very brilliant' (Vanessa to Roger Fry, 7 September 1924).

Moreover, where the paper succeeded was in occasionally managing to enlist the aid of Aunt Virginia - although even here we ran into unexpected difficulties. I was amazed to discover that she, a professional, seemed to have the greatest difficulty in writing. While I would draw pictures with the greatest ease, she would sit with a pen in her hand writing nothing, accusing me of being a brute and a slave-driver. Today I am able to see what she meant.

The room had one great advantage over all the others. Through the window you could step out onto the flat roof and to other roofs beyond. Sometimes when arguments became too fierce or the adventures of life too formidable, the roof was the best means of escape. This was Julian's favourite sport as well as being a road to freedom for, with courage and ingenuity, he could descend to the lane and escape altogether. From the spare room window one can see the coal shed roof on which Julian planted a house leek which still flourishes.

VN   In the 1930s the room was made over to guests. Its furniture is the usual assortment typical of Charleston: non-matching, eclectic and of variable quality. In 1936 Vanessa decided the room could do with a facelift; in April of that year she wrote to Julian: 'You won't be surprised to hear that I started the week here doing a little housepainting . . . Angelica and I decided that it would be fun to tackle the spare room. We have great plans for letting ourselves go in that, on the consideration that no visitor ever stays long enough to let it get on their nerves (or ought to do so) and we intend to introduce a fantastic note. But we haven't started yet.'

The washstand was hurriedly introduced when the elderly Dorothy Bussy came to stay after the war; it was probably decorated with the seashell design by Duncan in about 1946. Above the bed is Still Life with Plaster Head, *1947, by Vanessa. The components of the composition are still at Charleston. Over the washstand is* Still Life with Omega Cat, *1918, by Edward Wolfe. The cat in this painting was a ceramic one made by Henri Gaudier-Brzeska for the Omega Workshops. Vanessa painted the portrait of Chattie Salaman which hangs next to the window in 1940.*

Previous pages *The room is west-facing and rather dark until evening, but the window with its spectacular decorations done by Vanessa gives a dazzle of colour and light at one end. On the windowsill stands a glazed terracotta bust of a woman by Quentin, c. 1960 - what he would have described as 'one of my girls'. The vase was made at Foley's by Quentin in the late 1930s. It bears stripes of different colours, which have the names of the pigment written onto them. They serve as tests for ceramic paint, which often emerges completely altered by the firing process. Quentin used it for reference when working in the pottery.*

Above left *The dressing table incorporating a mirror had belonged to Julia Stephen, Vanessa's mother, and once stood in her room at Hyde Park Gate. Virginia Woolf referred to it when she recalled her mother's death in 1895: 'Led by George with towels wrapped around us and given each a drop of brandy in warm milk to drink, we were taken into the bedroom . . . I remember the long looking-glass; with the drawers on either side . . . and the great bed on which my mother lay.'*

Above right *For some reason, one small Staffordshire ornament held a particular place in Quentin's memory. 'It used to be in the drawing room at Gordon Square - a handsome ceramic zebra, a thing at which I always looked with joy and with an anxiety lest its delicate legs should be broken by some accident; at the time of writing it is still intact and stands on a shelf in the spare room at Charleston.'*

Opposite *The decorations of the spare room were a 1936 collaboration between Vanessa and Angelica, who painted the cupboard door with an ethereal dancing nymph. In contrast, the rather more concrete design of the fire screen is Vanessa's work. The mantelshelf hanging is nineteenth-century canvas work and used to adorn the fireplace in Duncan's London studio, 8 Fitzroy Street. Over the child's chair hangs a pencil drawing by Nina Hamnett entitled The Charlady, 1943. Nina, a painter, writer and bohemian, had been employed by Roger Fry at the Omega Workshops. Vanessa painted the still life of plums in 1945. The table lamp base is ceramic, made by Quentin in the 1950s.*

A few days later she wrote: 'Angelica and I spent some days alone [at Charleston] - We more or less finished our spare room decorations . . . It often astonishes me that Angelica can bear not to exploit her talents as a painter and especially perhaps as a decorator . . . it will be a great waste if she doesn't. They are really very surprising indeed.'

As usual the artists were not inhibited by convention in their interior decoration techniques: strips of paper stippled in grey were pasted around the walls to create pilasters; between them the walls were painted lavender grey with the shape of an arch in pink, 'a colour for which Nessa had a weakness but which I personally never liked', wrote Angelica. 'On the wall it looked like cooked lobster, though it later paled to salmon.' Elements of fantasy are most apparent in the nymph disporting on the cupboard door - this is Angelica's most individual contribution to the house's decorations - and also in the firescreen, the door and the window embrasure, all Vanessa's work.

My mother Olivier, who slept in this room in the early 1950s before her marriage to Quentin, recalls that at seven each morning she would hear the thump of Grace's footsteps descending the staircase which ran from her attic apartment directly behind the intervening spare room wall, against which the beds now stand. At eight o'clock Grace would knock on the door and appear bearing an enamel jug of hot water, which she placed on the washstand. Then, with a friendly comment on the day's weather, she would draw the curtains and leave the sleepy guest to rise and wash.

Being a visitor at Charleston was for many people over the years a heady experience. Frances Partridge tried to evoke her impressions of staying as a guest in the house: 'Charleston in its heyday [was] an enchanted place - a place of such potent individuality that whenever I stayed there I came away grateful to it, as it were, for giving me so much pleasure, so many rich and varied visual sensations, such *talk*, such an awareness that lives were being intensely and purposefully led there - for being *itself* in fact, just as one feels grateful to a very pretty girl for ravishing one's eyes.' (From a paper given at the Victoria and Albert Museum in 1985, reprinted in *Charleston Past and Present*.)

Above *The door panels were decorated by Vanessa - the cross-hatched surrounds are typical of her decorative style. Henri Doucet, a friend of Duncan and Vanessa's who worked at the Omega Workshops and was killed in World War One, painted the rather girlish portrait of Julian aged five, when he came to stay at Asheham House in 1911.*

Opposite *Vanessa and Angelica created the arch and pilaster effect on the walls in 1936. The pillared bookcase was decorated by Duncan in the 1920s. On top are a pair of Spanish vases. Above it hangs New House Farm, a painting by Duncan, 1920, given to Mr Hecks, the farmer near Firle who employed him and David Garnett as labourers during World War One when they were conscientious objectors. Mr Hecks was a humane employer and this gift was in recognition of his kindness. Either side are Still Life with Pears and Everlasting Flowers, c. 1945, by Vanessa, and White Roses, 1921, by her old friend Keith Baynes.*

The Garden

VN Gardens by their nature are changeable, and the restoration of the Charleston garden was an undertaking which begged all kinds of questions - of taste, memory and fact. Paintings, photographs, correspondence and memories were all ransacked to provide evidence of how the garden used to look. Sir Peter Shepheard was in charge of this prodigious undertaking, masterminding every aspect of the garden's restoration, from the rebuilding of the flint wall itself to the replanting of Vanessa's favourite hollyhocks. My father was never a horticulturist. As his memories show, he looked for pleasures other than plants in a garden. When the family arrived at Charleston in 1916, Virginia Woolf's description of it as 'a charming garden . . . now run rather wild' was certainly an understatement, and the 'grown-ups' may well have despaired of it. But for Julian and Quentin it offered unimaginable freedom.

QB The garden was divided into two parts: firstly the walled garden which was at that time a kitchen garden and which contained, when I first knew it, little save an ocean of mud and a few apple trees. It seemed a desolate place, where efforts had been made to cultivate potatoes. Secondly, there was the garden proper, in front of the house, which had been made 'respectable' with lawns and bushes. Beyond the lawn lay the pond and it was here that Julian and I began our activities in the spring of 1917.

The walled garden in high summer is a dense mass of flowers, overwhelming in their variety of colour. This is a painters' garden, and like the house was not intended to be tasteful or restrained. It is as though the exuberant decoration of the interior has spilled through the doors. Sir Peter Shepheard, who was in charge of the restoration, has described it as 'an apotheosis of the traditional English cottage garden'.

The pond was considerably larger and deeper than it is now. It was the home of carp and eels and sometimes, as summer drew on, of naked children. On it floated a punt. It was bounded on two shores by a wall of brick and flint, and on the further side by shallows and a supply of fresh water from a subterranean conduit. This ran beneath the field across the way to be fed by a spring, which in effect kept both the house and the farm supplied with water.

We were attracted to the pond because it was a natural place for activities in which the punt could play its part as the *Argo*, the *Santa Maria* or whatever else might be required. This protean vessel usually lay on the side of the pond nearest to the house, the side that was bounded by the wall. This was our harbour and it was named 'Varplise', a youthful corruption of Valparaiso.

On the other side of the pond there were other delights. The subterranean conduit debouched upon a gentle slope which reached out into the pond in such a way as to create the most beautifully geographical delta that any child could wish for. After a heavy rainfall, the main stream would overflow its banks and escape in dozens of minor rivulets. These meandered in a most attractive fashion to form low promontories which extended into the pond itself and could be adorned with artificial conduits, lakes, pools, docks, harbours and fortifications. This area - the 'River' as we called it - became the scene of many games and fantasies, a harbour for miniature navies, a place for childish engineering and a theatre of war.

The open space in the middle of the orchard was large enough to accommodate a place where a kind of tennis could be played with quoits hurled across a net; it was the one more or less customary game played at Charleston. Out in the fields Julian and I played what we called 'golf'; we each had a ball and the aim was to propel it across a field faster than one's brother. It was a much more energetic game than its namesake which I have never played and - for some snobbish reason I suppose - find detestable.

In the orchard all attempts to maintain respectability had been abandoned; nettles and rank grass grew high around the fruit trees. One of these grew the most delicious little round pears; from another we used to pick lovely little red apples called quarandines. But it was nearly a wilderness. In the middle of this dense thicket there was a kind of lair. One day in the summer of 1919 I wandered into the orchard and found Mr Keynes sitting there comfortably in his Rhoorkee chair with a great many documents beside him meditating the follies of Clemenceau, Wilson and Lloyd George and the likely state of post-war Europe. He told me he was going to France. 'Why?' I asked. 'For the Peace Conference,' he replied. 'And what will you say to them?' I enquired. 'I shall tell them that the Germans can't pay more money than they have.' Like nearly everything that Maynard said it sounded reasonable and indeed unanswerable.

The life that we led at Charleston was determined by the efforts of Vanessa to keep us under control and to give us some kind of education. But if the grown-ups had known some of the things that went on in our part of the garden, they would have been horrified. Like many boys we were atrociously cruel to animals and did a number of abominable things. There were also some less guilty but more dangerous enterprises. Julian somehow became possessed of a collection of bronze cannons. In those days it was astonishingly easy to obtain gunpowder, so we were able to load our artillery. After a couple of misfires I succeeded in lighting it. Bang! An enormous cloud of dense white smoke and no sign of our missile. Nor was there any sign of the cannon; it had shot backwards and buried itself in a garden bed.

Another experiment, which we did not repeat, involved one of those objects with which in those days you could make soda water, called a 'sparklet bulb'. This was a steel capsule containing carbonic acid gas. We once put gunpowder into an empty sparklet and cooked it on a bonfire, until, with a fearful noise, it exploded. We found the distorted fragments of the steel capsule deeply embedded in the trunk of an apple tree.

Above '*In summer Julian and Quentin often went naked, adding their beauty to the Charleston flowers and orchard. They would scramble over Maynard, ride each other horseback and fall into the pond. Vanessa sometimes followed them about stealthily, a Kodak in her hand. Duncan painted them*' (David Garnett in Flowers of the Forest, 1955). *When this picture was taken in 1925, the side of the pond bordering the lane was open, so that cows and horses could come to drink there each evening. It is now overgrown with trees.*

Right *The leaning female figure on the far side of the pond was made by Quentin in 1954. 'She has no name,' he wrote, 'but has been mistaken for a ghost by at least one impressionable guest.'*

VN Julian and Quentin were both pyromaniacs. One of their favourite games as children consisted of building a city out of newspaper and paste, complete with houses, churches and fortifications, which they then bombarded with lighted torches, a splendid sport which left rather a mess. I too remember playing this game as a child on the front gravel terrace at Charleston, under the enthusiastic guidance of my father.

Duncan, who appears to have led a more or less charmed life, nevertheless nearly incinerated himself on the occasion of one of Quentin's birthdays. In charge of the firework display over Charleston pond, Duncan accidentally knocked a bucket of petrol into the water, which he then set light to. The surface of the pond was a mass of flame, but Duncan escaped unharmed.

Bunny Garnett had a more scientific approach to the natural world: 'He talked to us about nature so that we got a rudimentary notion of what there was to be seen in the countryside around us.' Under his guidance, Julian and Quentin developed into reasonably knowledgeable, not to say ingenious, naturalists. In those days, before modern farming methods wrought havoc with the ecology of the downs, they were alive with an abundance of butterflies. Following a Stephen family tradition of 'bug-hunting', Quentin and his brother would set out saucers of treacle in the evenings and return the next morning to discover swarms of fascinating lepidoptera stuck fast in their traps. The boys impaled the best specimens and displayed them in a cabinet with glass-topped drawers.

When he took his own children to Charleston for the summer holidays, Quentin taught us how to make an 'Ant Palace', which consisted of two vertical sheets of glass fixed into wood at either end, between which one shovelled the earthy contents of an anthill and its inhabitants. This 'palace' was placed in a tray of water and the trapped ants, having nowhere to go, were clearly visible through the glass in their subterranean tunnels.

Quentin remembered how every year the house martins built beneath the eaves of the house a series of those hanging nests which are beautifully contrived to admit their owners and nothing larger. However, sometimes a party of 'rough insensitive sparrows' would invade a nest while it was still unfinished and evict the rightful inhabitants. Did one take sides? It was a moral problem which perplexed Quentin as a boy. An air gun would bring speedy retribution on the intruders, but was punishment justifiable? I don't believe he ever solved that question. Naughty and rowdy though he may have been, Quentin appears to have been a child with a strong grasp of right and wrong. He was thoughtful, impressionable, and easily upset.

QB The front lawn was bounded on one side by the pond and on the other side was a low wall with a rounded coping on which a daring child could run. The curve of the wall swept round to meet the curve of the pond at a holly bush, making a grassy corner which I associate with a youthful aesthetic experience. I had been lying there reading *Lambs' Tales from Shakespeare* and had struck King Lear. I came to the end and was deeply perturbed; I should have known better even then, but somehow I had imagined that stories end happily. Lear doesn't. It seemed all wrong. And yet at heart, I felt without at all being able to explain it, the beauty of a story in which it is the good who are punished.

On the other hand I still remember with what pleasurable excitement I lay on the grass beside the pond and read an account of the court of Kublai Khan. But the most memorable book was *Alice in Wonderland*. Vanessa read this to us one summer evening in the walled garden and I remember actually crying with laughter.

VN It took time for the walled garden to be transformed from a sea of mud and potatoes into the chaos of colour it is today. Life in wartime Sussex seemed to Vanessa principally a matter of survival, and the garden provided the household with the necessities of life. In 1917 she wrote to Roger Fry: 'I'm making great efforts to get hold of a pig, rabbits etc, and get the garden dug. I see the only way is to take complete charge myself' (Vanessa to Roger Fry, 22 February 1917).

But towards the end of the war her thoughts began to turn to improving the garden. As with so many things at Charleston, the architect of its new design was Roger Fry. He adopted what he saw as rational aesthetic principles in the restructuring of the walled garden, enclosing a rectangular lawn and pool with a grid of straight paths. By then, practicalities such as the growing of vegetables did not figure in his calculations.

Lessons in the Orchard, *painted by Duncan in 1917, shows Julian and Quentin with their nurse Mabel Selwood, who had been elevated by Vanessa to the position of governess. She was the first of several who attempted to educate the unruly Bell boys.*

Roger made designs quite early on, probably in 1917. Here, at the end of the war, the first steps were taken to transform this *hortus conclusus*. Flower beds intersected by gravel paths were established; a lawn bordered with cotton lavender containing a small pool was laid out; box hedges, roses, red-hot pokers and most strikingly those vast thistles, the globe artichokes which provided food at one season and props for still-lives at another, were planted. By the early twenties the garden was starting to flourish, to Vanessa's great delight: 'We have lots of apples, pears and even peaches, the best I have ever eaten from our own tree, planted ourselves 3 years ago! Doesn't that make your mouth water?' (Vanessa to Roger Fry, 9 September 1921).

In 1926 she wrote to Roger: 'It's so divine here now one can't bear leaving . . . The garden is full of dahlias and red admirals and one can sit out all day if one likes' (Vanessa to Roger Fry, September 1926).

Both Vanessa and Duncan were enthusiastic and practical gardeners, though they sometimes found themselves embroiled in arguments during which Duncan caused utter confusion by using the word perennials instead of annuals. Maynard Keynes, a dutiful guest, was known to help with the gardening. 'One would often find Maynard on the gravel path at the front of the house kneeling like a muslim on his prayer mat and, with enormous thoroughness, weeding a small patch of pathway with a penknife.'

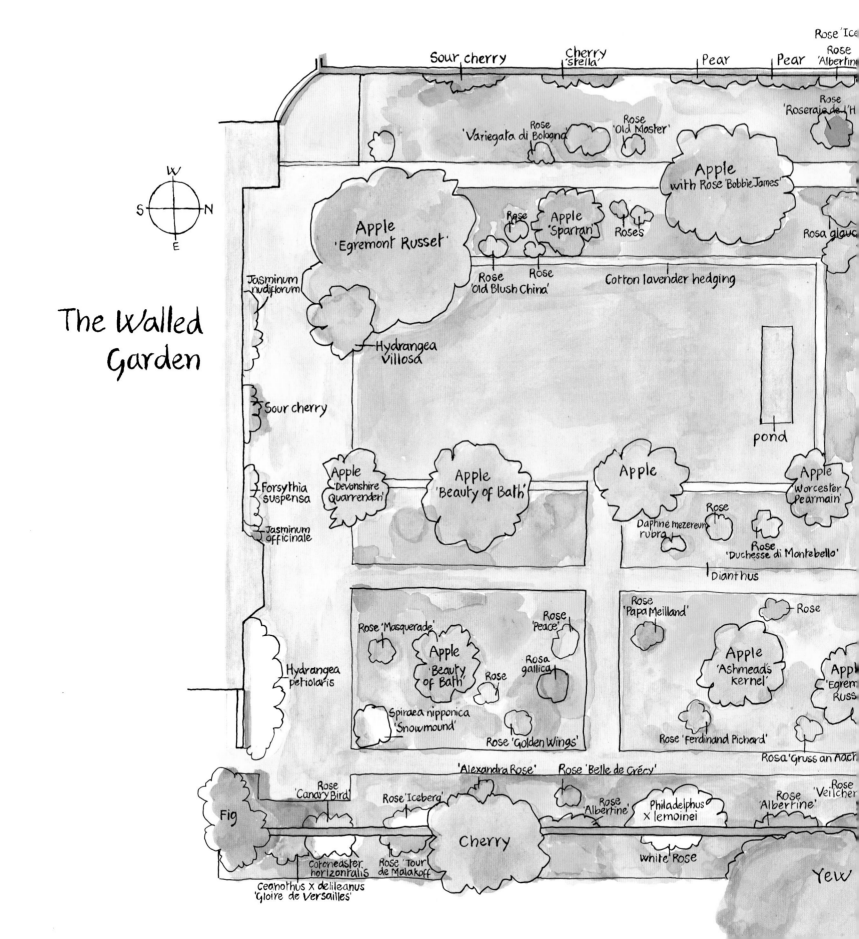

The Walled Garden

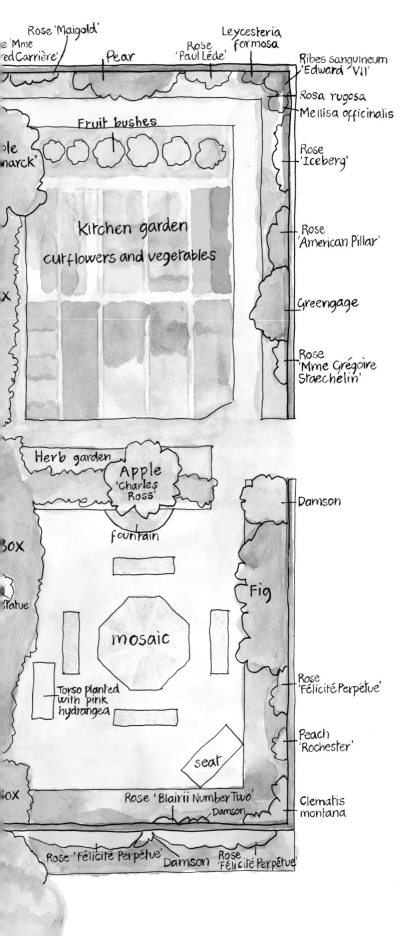

Rose 'Maigold'
'Mme
ed Carrière'
Pear
Rose 'Paul Léde'
Leycesteria formosa
Ribes sanguineum 'Edward VII'
Rosa rugosa
Mellisa officinalis

le
narck'

Fruit bushes

Rose 'Iceberg'

x

Kitchen garden
cutflowers and vegetables

Rose 'American Pillar'

Greengage

Rose 'Mme Grégoire Staechelin'

Herb garden

Apple 'Charles Ross'

Damson

Box

fountain

Statue

Fig

mosaic

Torso planted with pink hydrangea

Rose 'Félicité Perpétue'

Peach 'Rochester'

seat

Box

Rose 'Blairii Number Two'
Damson

Clematis montana

Rose 'Félicité Perpétue'
Damson
Rose 'Félicité Perpétue'

Left *In Duncan's old age, the upkeep of the walled garden became too demanding; paths and flower beds were laid to grass and it became largely neglected. However, many of the original shrubs, trees and perennials survived. These were retained when in 1986 Sir Peter Shepheard restored the garden to Roger Fry's original layout, replanting the flower beds with varieties which Duncan and Vanessa would have chosen in the 1930s. Many of these were annuals, and the garden now changes every summer, but always reflects Duncan and Vanessa's love for a rich mixture of colours and plants.*

Overleaf left *The layout of the walled garden is more clearly visible in spring, when the gravel paths between the borders and the small lawn are less dominated by tall growth. The apple tree here replaces an old Beauty of Bath which died. 'This bore apples', wrote Quentin, 'such as you might find in a child's picture book, yellow and vermilion, round, big and splendid; they tasted of cotton wool.'*

Overleaf right *The garden in spring. 'The buds all forming in the fruit trees but no blossom yet. It's a lovely moment, much more so than in the summer and I wish I could paint it.' (Vanessa to Julian Bell 29 March 1936) Clockwise from top left: Parrot tulips; Dutch irises; forget-me-nots; white Triumphator tulips.*

Left *Vanessa took this group photograph in 1921; from the left, Leonard Woolf, with Quentin as a fat boy of eleven on his lap; Julian, with Maynard Keynes standing behind him; Mary Hutchinson in the hammock; Clive and Duncan.*

Right *In later years the box hedges in the garden grew out of control. Today they are clipped to prevent further growth, but the geometrical severity of the original hedges cannot be recaptured without killing them by severe pruning. The modest lady in their midst is a cast of a Giovanni da Bologna. Vanessa and Duncan collected numerous art school casts (Clive complained that walking round the garden was like being assailed by familiar quotations), but unfortunately they never learnt to protect them from the weather, so most perished.*

Although Vanessa enjoyed pruning and weeding, and Duncan loved choosing plants, on the whole the hard work was left to the gardener. For many years he was a melancholy but sympathetic old man known as Young Mr Stevens, since although he was a pensioner his mother, the wife of Old Mr Stevens, lived to be nearly a hundred. In later years the gardening was done by Grace Higgens's husband, Walter, who grew vegetables for the household in the plot to the north of the walled garden.

Because Charleston was for much of the time the family's holiday home, the garden was created to be enjoyed mainly in the summer months. The lawn was surrounded by flower borders scented with tobacco plants and old-fashioned pinks, dazzling with dahlias and zinnias and loud with the buzzing of bees. Vanessa and Duncan's choice of flowers reflected their love of colour, of Bonnard and Matisse. This was and is a painter's garden. In the summer of 1930 Vanessa wrote to Roger: 'the garden . . . is incredibly beautiful, though Helen [Anrep, with whom Roger Fry lived], wouldn't like it, as it's full of reds of all kinds, scabious & hollyhocks & mallows & every kind of red from red lead to black. Pokers are coming out. It's all in very good order & we have masses of plums and apples. I have of course begun by painting some flowers, it seems the inevitable way to begin here' (Vanessa to Roger Fry, 6 August 1930).

A week later she wrote again: 'I'm painting flowers - one can't resist them - I don't want to gloat over Helen's garden but really when the sun comes out once in a blue moon you can't conceive what the medley of apples, hollyhocks, plums, zinnias, dahlias, all mixed up together is like' (Vanessa to Roger Fry, 15 Aug 1930).

It was a delight for Vanessa to see her garden become a haven for her children and their friends: 'I must say it has been rather amazing here this week,' she wrote to Julian in 1936. 'The house seems full of young people in very high spirits, laughing a great deal at their own jokes . . . lying about in the garden which is simply a dithering blaze of flowers and butterflies and apples.'

Above *Duncan and Angelica in the walled garden in 1927 are dwarfed by the vast snaking heads of red-hot pokers. Angelica's memories, and photographs such as these, were invaluable evidence when the garden was restored in the 1980s.*

Left *Summer flowers in the walled garden include tobacco plants, campanula and cornflowers and a silver cotton thistle which has self-seeded. Vanessa and Duncan loved the subtlety of silver foliage.*

Right *Lining the path as one enters the walled garden are foxgloves, opium poppies, an iceberg rose, self-seeded Shirley poppies and orange anthemis.*

Overleaf *At the height of summer marigolds, opium poppies, 'Ladybird' poppies, foxgloves, feverfew, campanula, Shirley poppies, cornflowers, alliums, white yarrow, pink geraniums, roses, lilies, anthemis, echinops thistle and borage are all in flower.*

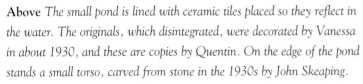

Above *The small pond is lined with ceramic tiles placed so they reflect in the water. The originals, which disintegrated, were decorated by Vanessa in about 1930, and these are copies by Quentin. On the edge of the pond stands a small torso, carved from stone in the 1930s by John Skeaping.*

Above right *Theatricals in the walled garden in 1935. The performers are, from left to right, Julian, Janie Bussy, Angelica and Quentin. This performance was a verse drama about Damon and Phyllis written by Angelica (who had theatrical ambitions). However, she suffered from stage fright on this occasion owing to the fact that George Rylands, well known as a director at the Arts Theatre, Cambridge, was in the audience.*

Left *Quentin wrote of the Giovanni da Bologna cast: 'She is only a cast, and casts have a bad name. Indeed the massacre of the casts is one of the tragedies of modern art education.' Newly unwrapped from her winter frost protection, this one survives to see the spring in a corner of the walled garden beneath an overhanging apple tree.*

The site of the central lawn, with its gentle slopes descending to the small rectangular pool, made the perfect auditorium, 'a capital scene for theatrical performances'. Some of these theatricals are captured in Vanessa's photographs; they were performed by the 'children' for the 'grown-ups', though Quentin remembered being well into his twenties at the time of one of them. Their subject matter appears to have been vaguely mythological, with a sprinkling of 'ladies dying of love'. Angelica proved able to compose yards of heroic verse, but they were not intended to be serious.

QB Duncan once told me that his idea of a garden was something exotic. It should be a kind of island, as different as possible from its surroundings. He could well have been describing the walled garden, but he was in fact speaking of Grant's Folly, the little garden behind the studio which consists of a small enclosure devoted mainly to fig trees, with a square pool in the middle, surrounded by gravel. A vine, which has spread across the studio roof and the pergola on the other side, shades the entrance to the studio. It is indeed very unlike the surrounding Sussex meadows.

Left *'It has been so hot one could hardly go into the garden even, but rather delicious, and the Piazza with running water in it at its most Piazza-like' (Vanessa to Angelica Garnett, 23 July 1958). The tiny semi-circular pool and its spouting head, both made by Quentin, were added to the Piazza in 1958. Their inauguration was celebrated with champagne. The water is now barely visible beneath waterlilies, flag irises and overhanging salvias.*

Right *Panels of broken crockery, like stained-glass windows, have been incorporated into the floor of the Piazza. In this suntrap, completely sheltered by walls, Mediterranean plants such as figs and sages thrive in the reflected heat. The lower half of a female figure was once a whole torso which stood beside the pond in the lawn. It was accidentally pushed in and broken by Quentin's young son Julian, but was retrieved by Duncan, who ingeniously converted it into a planter for hydrangeas.*

Quentin left many marks upon the physical appearance of the garden. In 1946 he devised the 'Piazza'. It took him nearly a year to construct in concrete and brick, and it was a rather unequal collaboration: 'I reserved large areas for the painters and they did the mosaics.' These were made out of broken china resulting from household disasters. Here stood the portable garden seat on which Duncan collapsed from tedium in the company of Dame Ethel Smyth. The pool was made by Quentin, who had a mania for ponds which was to remain with him all his life. He never had a garden into which he did not contrive to bring water, whether just to create those reflections so beloved of the painters, to swim in, to keep fish, or sometimes all three. Inspired by the Generalife Gardens in Granada, Quentin set out to run a channel of water from the house across the walled garden descending to the pool in the lawn, and another channel running from that pool to join the lower pool in the Piazza. As the water supply for this project was simply a tap in the house, the result was disappointing. There is no sign of it today. Undeterred, Quentin then dreamed up a cunning plan to divert excess water from the farm dairy across the road, run it through an underground channel and through a hole in the banks of the pond in front of the house where it would emerge pure and crystalline, thus cleansing the pond. Unfortunately his water source turned out to be the water used for sluicing out the cowsheds, thus defeating his purpose.

Quentin's final attempt at water engineering came with the digging of what he hoped would be a swimming pool, which was supposed to fill with overflow water from the pond.

At the north-east corner of the pond there are still traces of what Clive called 'Quentin's Dell', which mark his unfinished excavations. At the end of the orchard path is a grove of yew trees and there stands a sculpted figure with a bucket of fruit on her head, known as 'Pomona'. Behind the yews is set a pedestal of bricks upon which is seated a lady, carved in brick, and popularly known as the 'Spink', a name gratefully accepted by her creator.

QB I began work on the Spink in 1930. Somebody had told me about the brick sculptures at Vallombrosa, and this was what set me off. I went to the bottom of the garden and began to design and measure up the base of my sculpture. It would be - and I think this can still be quite clearly seen in the colossal remains that still exist - a vast cubic monument, which would finally become a seated female figure. I worked pretty hard at the base, and the base is in fact the only really decent part of the job today.

It had some charm, and some virtue considering my complete ignorance of all the arts of bricklaying. The material was really impossible; nobody had told me how to choose my bricks - I hadn't enquired - and I was forever running into the middle of the brick, which was so friable, so full of lumps of stone, anthracite, heaven knows what, that I was unable to make any shape out of it at all. It has now become one of the oddities of Charleston and, for all I know, some people may even take it seriously as a work of art.

VN Taking himself seriously as an artist was something Quentin was disinclined to do. He would have laughed with exasperation at some of the interpretations attributed to his sculpture of a floating lady who lies, supported only by her hair, her horizontal form reflected in the pond - 'Two for the price of one' as he would say. In fact Quentin's imagination had been stimulated at an early age by a visit with his Uncle Adrian and Aunt Karin to a magic show at Maskelyne and Cook's, where the magician's beautiful assistant lay down upon a table and was covered with a sheet. The magician then levitated her until she lay horizontal and rigid about

Below *Quentin's Spink was made in 1930. 'The name has stuck rather better than the brickwork,' he wrote.*

Left *Against a background of yew at the end of the orchard stands Pomona. She was constructed from concrete by Quentin in 1954; the apples in the bucket on her head are made from glazed terracotta.*

Opposite left *The flint and brick wall is surmounted by a row of casts of antique heads. Over the years most of them have crumbled and this Antinous is a replacement.*

Opposite right *Quentin made the levitating figure in 1973, a grand undertaking which I remember well. Finished to resemble bronze, the secret of her gravity-defying pose is her construction from moulded fibreglass concealing a rigid armature.*

six feet from the floor. 'I was dumbfounded: the thing was impossible. The orchestra echoed my feelings with a roll of drums, and then I was further dumbfounded. The magician with one masterly twitch of his hand withdrew the sheet and revealed - absolutely nothing. She had vanished into thin air.' Years later Quentin began to construct levitating sculptures which gradually, over time, assumed a female form. 'Then I realised that it was that disappearing lady seen and missed so long ago at Maskelyne and Cook's.'

The garden was as full of associations and memories for Quentin as the house. In 1936 his brother Julian returned from two years spent at Wuhan University in China, determined upon a more active role in the political events that were unfolding in Europe:

QB   There is a path at Charleston which leads up beside the walled garden to the gravel in front of the house. On the one side you have the pond, on the other the wall with whatever collection of good old art-school props Duncan might have collected - the Hermes of Praxiteles, the Venus de Medici, the dying gladiator, all in plaster, pitted by the rain and sometimes so much worn away that one might find a cavity big enough to house a thrush and its brood. Here Julian and I walked up and down. He had come back from China, leaving some domestic tangle still unknotted, and talked about his plans. Should he, or should he not go and fight in Spain? The decision was made; Julian left for Spain and in July 1937 came news of his death. Vanessa was completely shattered.

We took her back to Charleston and for the rest of that summer Virginia devoted herself completely to her sister and gradually restored her to a quiet and very sad convalescence. On one of the few days when she could not come over to Charleston, Virginia sent her sister a note. I found Vanessa quietly crying over it in the garden. 'Another love letter from Virginia,' she smiled very faintly.

Vanessa's idea for a monument to Julian did not turn out very well. She decided to plant a row of poplars just outside the walled garden. They were to replace the noble line of elms which once stood in the field to the west of the house and which, during the past few years, had been dying one by one. The new trees were planted but they did not flourish. They are all gone now.

Above *Vanessa in 1960, seated on the terrace in front of the house.*

Opposite *'How extraordinary that there should be such an unchanged spot in the world still,' wrote Janie Bussy of the Charleston garden in 1947. After thirty years of Bloomsbury occupancy it was then in its maturity, a teeming mass of flowers. Today the summer borders still spill over with geraniums, delphiniums and poppies.*

VN   Angelica has described Charleston as 'an earthly Paradise'. I was fortunate in spending my own summer holidays as a child at Charleston and I think I know what she means. If Paradise was a garden then the garden at Charleston may well be its Platonic shadow. When Vanessa painted her Annunciation in Berwick Church, two miles away, she did not have to look far for models. In that church, she and Duncan fulfilled an ambition to paint walls as the artists of the Quattrocento had done. Here, Vanessa's Virgin Mary is Angelica, and true to Renaissance iconography she kneels before the Angel Gabriel in a garden - but this one is walled with flint, pathed with gravel and edged with grey-green lavender. Her Madonna lilies were probably culled from Vanessa's own borders. The garden is Charleston and Vanessa's painting is a celebration of her private Heaven.

Suggested Further Reading

Anscombe, Isabelle *Omega and After* Thames and Hudson, London, 1981

Bell, Clive *Old Friends: Personal Recollections* Chatto & Windus, London, 1956

Bell, Quentin, Angelica Garnett, Henrietta Garnett and Richard Shone *Charleston Past and Present* Hogarth Press, London, revised edition 1993

Bell, Quentin *Bloomsbury* Weidenfeld and Nicolson, London, new edition 1986
Virginia Woolf, A Biography Hogarth Press, London, 1972
Elders and Betters John Murray, London, 1995

Bell, Quentin, and Angelica Garnett *Vanessa Bell's Family Album* Jill Norman and Hobhouse Ltd, London, 1981

Charleston Guide Notes published by The Charleston Trust 1996

Collins, Judith *The Omega Workshops* Secker & Warburg, London, 1983

Dunn, Jane *A Very Close Conspiracy: Vanessa Bell and Virginia Woolf* Jonathan Cape, London, 1990

Garnett, Angelica *Deceived with Kindness* Chatto & Windus, The Hogarth Press, London, 1984

Garnett, David *The Flowers of the Forest* Chatto & Windus, London, 1955

Holroyd, Michael *Lytton Strachey: A Critical Biography* Heineman, London, 1967; revised edition Vintage [Random House] 1995

Lee, Hugh (ed) *A Cézanne in the Hedge* Collins and Brown, London, 1992

MacWeeney, Alen, and Sue Allison *Bloomsbury Reflections* WW Norton, New York; Ryan, London, 1990

Marler, Regina (ed) *Selected Letters of Vanessa Bell* Bloomsbury, London; Pantheon, New York, 1993

Naylor, Gillian (ed) *Bloomsbury: The Artists, Authors and Designers by themselves* Pyramid Books [Reed Consumer Books], London, 1990; Mitchell Beazley [Reed Consumer Books], London, 1993

Rosenbaum, S.P. (ed) *The Bloomsbury Group (Memoirs and Commentary)* University of Toronto Press, revised edition 1995

Shone, Richard *Bloomsbury Portraits* Phaidon Press, London, 1993

Skidelsky, Robert *John Maynard Keynes* (2 vols) Macmillan, London, 1983, 1992

Spalding, Frances *Vanessa Bell* Weidenfeld and Nicolson, London, 1983
Duncan Grant Chatto & Windus, London, 1997

Sutton, Denys (ed) *Letters of Roger Fry* (2 vols) Chatto & Windus, London, 1972

Watney, Simon *The Art of Duncan Grant* John Murray, London, 1990

Woolf, Virginia *Moments of Being: Unpublished Autobiographical Writings* edited by Jeanne Schulkind 2nd edition, Hogarth Press, London, 1985
The Letters of Virginia Woolf (6 vols) edited by Nigel Nicolson and Joanne Trautmann Banks, Hogarth Press, London, 1975-80
The Diary of Virginia Woolf (5 vols) edited by Anne Olivier Bell, Hogarth Press, London, 1977-84

The Charleston Magazine: Charleston, Bloomsbury and the Arts published by the Charleston Trust, nos 1-15, 1990-97

The Charleston Newsletter edited by Hugh Lee, nos 1-24, published by the Charleston Trust 1982-89

Visiting Charleston

Charleston is open to the public between April and the end of October, on Wednesdays, Thursdays, Fridays, Saturdays, Sundays and Bank Holiday Mondays, from 2pm to 6pm. The last entry is at 5pm. In July and August the house is open from 11.30am to 6pm. The house may be unsuitable for children under eight years old. For further visitor information telephone 0 (44) 1323 811265.

Charleston is 60 miles/90 kilometres south of London and is signposted off the A27 between Brighton and Eastbourne. Trains from London run hourly to Lewes, six miles/nine kilometres away; from there it is advisable to take a taxi.

Berwick Church, which is decorated with murals by the Charleston artists, is two miles/three kilometres east of Charleston off the A27, and is open daily.

The Bloomsbury Workshop, which sells works by Bloomsbury artists, is at 12 Galen Place, London WC1A 2JR.

Index

Acknowledgements

Authors' Acknowledgements

On behalf of my late father and myself, I would like to thank the following people who have helped to make this book possible: Alastair Upton and the staff at Charleston, in particular Peter Miall the curator and Andrew Caverly the gardener; James Beechey; Richard Shone, historian of the Bloomsbury artists; Elizabeth Inglis of Sussex University Library; Angelica Garnett; Sir Peter Shepheard; Caroline Bugler, our editor at Frances Lincoln Publishers; and above all Olivier Bell.

Photographer's Acknowledgements

My warmest thanks go to Ray Roberts at Henry Holt and Anne Fraser, Caroline Hillier, Erica Hunningher, Trish Going, Louise Kirby and Caroline Bugler at Frances Lincoln. I would also like to thank those at Charleston, especially Myra Harud and Eve Lancaster, and many others who helped me with the photography there; Davy Jones for his tireless and invaluable assistance and Scouse humour; Hazel Hammond for her support; and Anthony Accardi for the excellence of his colour prints. It was an additional honour to have had Quentin Bell and his daughter Virginia Nicholson as the authors.

Publishers' Acknowledgements

Frances Lincoln Publishers would like to thank Ray Roberts at Henry Holt for introducing us to Alen MacWeeney and for interest at every stage; the Charleston Trust, without whose enthusiasm and involvement this book would not have been possible; and Tony Bradshaw of the Bloomsbury Workshop in London for his help and encouragement.

For assistance in creating the book, the Publishers are grateful to James Bennett, Hilary Mandleberg, Vanessa Fletcher, Fred Gill and Louise Kirby, and to Kathie Gill for the index.

Illustrations by Robert Campling
Colour prints by Anthony Accardi

Editor	Caroline Bugler
Editorial Assistant	Sarah Labovitch
Picture Editor	Sue Gladstone
Production	Vivien Antwi
Head of Pictures	Anne Fraser
Art Director	Caroline Hillier
Editorial Director	Erica Hunningher

Photographic Acknowledgements

For permission to reproduce the paintings and photographs on the following pages, and for supplying photographs, the Publishers thank those listed below.

(**A**=above, **B**=below, **L**=left, **R**=right)

9 Collection Bryan Ferry; 16,17,18,19 Tate Gallery Archive; 20 Private collection; 25 *Still Life with a Bookcase* (1919) by Duncan Grant, reproduced by courtesy of The British Council; 30 Tate Gallery Archive; 34 reproduced with the kind permission of the Trustees of the Ulster Museum, Belfast; 40 Corporate Art Collection, The Reader's Digest Association, Inc.; 45 The Charleston Trust; 50 reproduced by courtesy of the Provost and Scholars of King's College, Cambridge; 59 Williamson Art Gallery and Museum, Birkenhead; 60 Tate Gallery Archive; 62 The Charleston Trust; 70 The Bloomsbury Workshop; 75R The Charleston Trust; 79 Private collection; 85 Sheffield City Art Galleries/The Bridgeman Art Library; 89 Tate Gallery Archive; 91 Private collection; 96 Bust of Lytton Strachey by Stephen Tomlin, reproduced by courtesy of the Keatley Trust; 99L *Portrait of Vanessa Bell* (1942) by Duncan Grant, reproduced by courtesy of the Tate Gallery, London; 102 reproduced by courtesy of the Provost and Scholars of King's College, Cambridge; 112BL Tate Gallery Archive; 112R University of Sussex Library, Manuscripts Section; 126 Tate Gallery Archive; 129 The Charleston Trust; 134,137L,141R Tate Gallery Archive; 147 Private collection.

All paintings by Duncan Grant © Henrietta Garnett. All paintings by Vanessa Bell © Angelica Garnett.